Mysterious Monsters of the World

Vikas Khatri

PUSTAK MAHAL®
Delhi • Bangalore • Mumbai • Patna • Hyderabad

J-3/16 , Daryaganj, New Delhi-110002
☎ 23276539, 23272783, 23272784 • *Fax:* 011-23260518
E-mail: info@pustakmahal.com • *Website:* www.pustakmahal.com

Sales Centre

- 10-B, Netaji Subhash Marg, Daryaganj, New Delhi-110002
  ☎ 23268292, 23268293, 23279900 • *Fax:* 011-23280567
  E-mail: rapidexdelhi@indiatimes.com
- 6686, Khari Baoli, Delhi-110006
  ☎ 23944314, 23911979

Branches

Bengaluru: ☎ 080-22234025 • *Telefax:* 080-22240209
E-mail: pustak@airtelmail.in • pustak@sancharnet.in
Mumbai: ☎ 022-22010941, 022-22053387
E-mail: rapidex@bom5.vsnl.net.in
Patna: ☎ 0612-3294193 • *Telefax:* 0612-2302719
E-mail: rapidexptn@rediffmail.com

ISBN 978-81-223-0959-3

Edition: 2012

Printed at : **Sharma Printers, Delhi**

Contents

Introduction

The world is full of uncatalogued animals and creatures that defy our imaginations. There has been an ongoing effort to find these mystery animals/creatures. This is the study of *Cryptozoology* (the study of hidden animals) established by Bernard Heuvelmans. Cryptozoologists search for animals that are thought to be extinct but still reported to be seen today, new creatures that are rarely seen and continue to elude the eye of man. Some of the creatures are well known legends such as *Bigfoot* and the *Loch Ness Monster,* but many other creatures are said to exist and are just as weird as the famous cases. Like any claims of unusual happenings, there is also a certain percentage of reports that are explained away as hoaxes. In fact, few are ever proven to be realistic animals and worthy of scientific classification. However, this is often NOT the fault of researchers. Some animals live outside the range of human exploration. Take for instance, the *Giant Squid.* While there is substantial reason to believe they exist, it is virtually impossible to find a live specimen because of the depths it resides in. It is a deep sea animal and so far, no deep sea equipment has been able to catch or film a live Giant Squid in its natural environment.

How then, can we evaluate the monsters mentioned in the pages of this book? We might conceive that there was some kind of 'probability scale' with a score of 10 for something certain to exist and a score of zero for something that does not. I have reached empirical conclusions as to the being or otherwise of a reported monster being what it claims to be, in the event the decision is yours.

We must be truly openminded while at the same time remembering the snare of having an open mind: people come along and dump things in it.

1. Yeti

Although the North American Bigfoot may be slightly more famous, the *Yeti* of the Himalayas probably merits distinction as the great-granddaddy of the missing links. The giant, dark-furred creature that leaves mammoth footprints in the snow has been described in the folklore of Nepal and Tibet for countless generations. Its name is derived from the Sherpa term *'yeh-teh'*, which loosely translates as "that-there thing."

The first European to encounter evidence of a Yeti was the British explorer L.A. Waddell, who saw large footprints in the snows on a Himalayan peak. But the creature would not become internationally known until 1921. An expedition led by Charles Kenneth Howard-Bury found footprints while climbing Mt. Everest, and Howard-Bury spotted distant dark figures through his binoculars. The explorer later told journalists that his Sherpa guides had called the creatures *'metoh-kangmi,'* a generic Nepalese term for mountain beasts. This word was accidentally mistranslated, and suddenly news reports were claiming that explorers had seen a man-monster the natives called the "abominable snowman."

The erroneous phrase had a certain ring that aroused people's imagination around the world, and the myth of the Yeti was instantly immortalised. The popularity of the "snowman" term probably helped generate the misconception that the Yeti has white fur, something like the Wampa snow beast in *The Empire Strikes Back,* when in fact most sightings specify that the creature has a coat of black or dark brown hair.

In 1951, mountaineer Eric Shipton, the leader of the Everest Reconnaissance Expedition, discovered a well-preserved giant footprint at 5,400 metres. It was longer than an axe handle, measuring 45 cm long by 30 cm wide, and appeared to bear only four toes, which were extremely broad.

In 1957, Texas oil millionaire Tom Slick launched a series of expeditions in search of the Yeti. Slick had an unabiding love for cryptozoology, and his money could buy him no greater thrill than the promise of bringing the abominable snowman into captivity. Slick's efforts were largely fruitless, except for a 1958 expedition that revealed the alleged bones of a Yeti's hand, an artifact enshrined at a monastery in Pangboche, Nepal.

The monks refused to let expedition member Peter Byrne remove the hand from the premises, but he hatched a plan to steal parts of it. In 1959, Byrne secretly switched human hand bones for the some of the bones of the Yeti hand, and he smuggled the Pangboche originals out of the country with the valuable assistance of Jimmy Stewart, the famed actor. Stewart just happened to be passing through India, and he and his wife

Gloria agreed to wrap up the stolen bones in their underwear inside their luggage.

Scientific analysis of the Pangboche bones was mixed. British primatologist Osman Hill initially announced that the bones were of human origin, but then he changed his mind and declared them unidentifiable as any known primate. Later he revised his opinion yet again, saying that the Pangboche hand must have belonged to a Neanderthal. Unfortunately, the smuggled bones were lost and cannot be re-examined today.

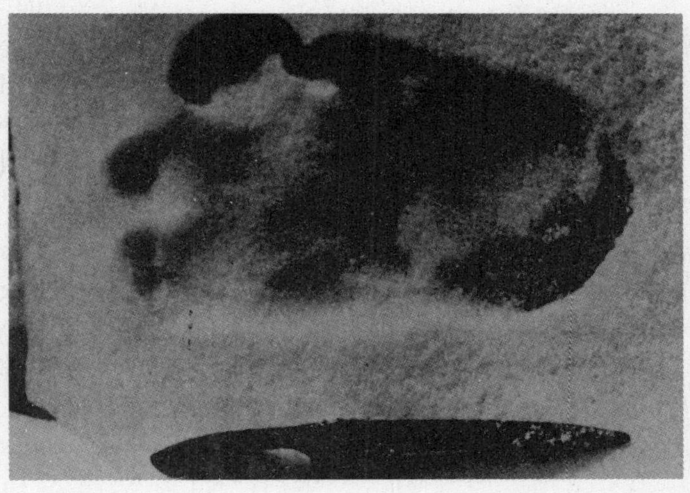

Sir Edmund Hillary's anti-Yeti crusade succeeded in letting some of the air out of the abominable snowman myth, but sightings continued periodically over the years, possibly re-invigorated somewhat by the Patterson Bigfoot film in 1967. One of the most dramatic Yeti encounters of all time was reported in 1974 by Lakpa Sherpani, a 19-year-old Nepalese girl. She was tending a herd of yaks alongside a stream near Mt. Everest when a dark-furred Yeti suddenly attacked. She said it killed several of her yaks, either by hitting them or breaking their necks by violently twisting their horns. The Yeti also grabbed her and knocked her unconscious.

At the other extreme, British mountain climber Anthony Wooldridge experienced one of the *least* dramatic Yeti encounters ever known, in 1986. Climbing the Himalayas, he observed some strange tracks in the snow, and later spotted an apparent dark-haired creature in the far distance. Wooldridge made his way to within about 150 m of the unmoving humanoid figure, and took photographs. He observed the creature intently for 45 minutes, and it never moved a muscle. Threatening weather forced Wooldridge to leave before the Yeti did.

Wooldridge's photographs, trumpeted as the first ever taken of a Yeti, were the object of intense public and scientific scrutiny. Famed zoologist Desmond Morris called the photos "puzzling," but allowed tentatively that the creature might be an abominable snowman.

2. Bigfoot

The furry man-monster of the North American continent has achieved such legendary status that the term *"Bigfoot"* is in danger of becoming a generic label applied to any big hairy creature that walks like a man. The following discussion will focus on the "original" Bigfoot, the seven-foot apelike beast sighted in the woods of the Pacific Northwest and in Canada, where it is traditionally known as *Sasquatch*.

Some Bigfoot hunters believe that the creature's earliest history can be found in ancient Native American legends, particularly in the tales of the Witiko, or Wendigo, a giant spirit-beast from the lore of the Algonkian tribe. Others argue that Bigfoot seems to be a 20th century phenomenon, and any earlier documentation of the creature's existence is tenuous at best. If Bigfoot has indeed been known to Native Americans for ages, it's only in the past hundred years that persons of European descent have begun to report seeing him.

During the 1900s, the *Colonist* newspaper in Victoria, British Columbia, ran several stories about people spotting "monkey-men" in remote wooded areas. In the 1920s, British Columbia schoolteacher J. W. Burns wrote extensively in newspaper and magazine articles about reports of giant hairy creatures. Burns's writings were responsible for popularising the term "Sasquatch," which he identified as a derivation from the language of the Coast Salish Indians. Sasquatch quickly became known among the general public of western Canada, long before tales of such a creature ever found notoriety in the United States.

Following the publicity surrounding Eric Shipton's 1951 photograph of a Yeti footprint, interest in Sasquatch increased dramatically. John Green, a newspaper publisher in British Columbia, began reporting Sasquatch sightings in 1955. Green initially intended this coverage to be purely a circulation booster for his small newspaper, and some of his reports were completely fake — such as an April Fool's story about Sasquatch kidnapping a young woman. But over time Green became genuinely captivated by the creature, and his extensive compilation of stories and sightings made him the leading Sasquatch authority of his day.

One Sasquatch spotter Green interviewed was William Roe, a trapper, who claimed to have a close encounter with a female of the species in 1955, while hunting on British Columbia's Mica Mountain.

"The thought came to me that if I shot it, I would probably have a specimen of great interest to scientists the world over," Roe said. But he couldn't bring himself to pull the trigger on his rifle. "Although I have called the creature 'it,' I felt now that it was a human being, and I knew I would never forgive myself if I killed it," he said.

The publication of Roe's account would later inspire another man to step forward with his own Sasquatch experience, which he said had happened more than thirty years before. Albert Ostman, a 64-year-old retired lumberman from British Columbia, went public in 1957 with a tale he had kept to himself since 1924, for fear of being ridiculed. Ostman's story was the most dramatic report ever in the history of Bigfoot studies: a first-person account of abduction by Sasquatch.

While on a camping trip near Vancouver Island, Ostman found that something had disturbed his supplies and food on two nights in a row. A Native American trail guide had warned him about the presence of local Sasquatches when Ostman set up his camp, and this was the first time Ostman had ever heard of the creatures, but he didn't think they could be the culprits messing with his gear.

Then one night, Ostman was shaken awake to find himself being indelicately carried away inside his sleeping bag. The opening of the sleeping bag was held shut, and Ostman had no choice but to be dragged along the forest ground for what he estimated to be 40 km, nearly suffocating. After what seemed like a three-hour ordeal, he was thrown to the ground in a heap, and emerged to find himself in the company of four Sasquatches. Ostman described them as a family, with a father and a mother and their pair of offspring, one male and one female. He indicated that the adult male, his kidnapper, was over 2.5 m tall and powerfully built, covered in dark hair all over. The children, though smaller, were still about 2 m tall.

Ostman said the Sasquatches chattered amongst themselves in a seemingly intelligent language, and although they did not hurt or threaten him, they were determined not to let him leave. Their lair was inside a small valley enclosed by cliffs, and the adult male stood guard at the only apparent entry passage. Ostman suggested that he may have been selected as a prospective mate for the young female!

Ostman claimed that he was held captive for a period of six days. In that time he formed a tentative bond with the younger male, who became fond of sampling Ostman's snuff. That gave Ostman an idea. He offered his snuff to the adult male, who impulsively dumped the entire container into his mouth. The tobacco rush incapacitated the big Sasquatch in short order, making him writhe on the ground in overwhelming discomfort. Ostman seized the opportunity to escape, and never told anyone his fantastic tale until three decades later, when it seemed the world might be ready to listen. As unbelievable as his story may seem, many of those who heard Ostman tell it firsthand remarked that his earnest demeanour made it come across as surprisingly convincing.

Ostman's "sleeping-bag snatch" remains the most elaborately detailed account of Bigfoot contact, but as any amateur cryptozoologist knows, it is far from the most famous sighting of the creature. That honour belongs to 952 frames of 16mm film, shot one fine day in the California woods.

Capturing the fleeting sight of a 2 m apelike creature retreating into the Northern California wilderness, the Patterson Bigfoot film is among the most renowned artifacts in the field of paranormal study. The footage has achieved iconic status even among the public at large, and forms the foundation of many Bigfoot hunters' beliefs.

The controversial reel of film was shot by Roger Patterson, a former rodeo rider who had become deeply fascinated with

Bigfoot after reading press reports about the creature in 1957. He wrote and self-published a book in 1966 entitled *Do Abominable Snowmen of America Really Exist?* Patterson then set out to film a documentary about sightings of Bigfoot.

On October 20, 1967, Patterson and his friend Bob Gimlin were riding on horseback in the wilds of California's Bluff Creek valley, with Patterson carrying a rented 16mm camera to shoot some atmospheric footage for his planned film. He ended up filming a lot more than just scenery. Patterson and Gimlin spotted a huge, dark-furred, bipedal creature hunched over in the middle of a creek. The beast rose to a full height that Patterson estimated at 2 m, and began walking toward the woods. Thrown to the ground after his horse reared up in fright, Patterson anxiously yanked the movie camera from his saddlebag and began shooting. The day's filming had left him with 9 m of film in the camera, but he managed to record the alleged Bigfoot's image briefly before it fled from view.

Patterson and Gimlin discovered that a number of footprints had been left behind, and they preserved them in plaster casts. The tracks were 35 cm and 12 cm wide. But these trophies were almost insignificant in comparison to the prize inside Patterson's camera.

In the ensuing three decades, the 952 frames of Patterson's Bigfoot film have been submitted to all manner of examination and analysis. The creature has been classified as female, because of its apparent breasts. Theorists have extrapolated descriptions of everything, from its psychological bearing to its eating habits on the basis of its behaviour in the film. Minutiae of the creature's physiognomy, such as the exact way in which it moves its neck, and its unusual method of distributing its weight as it strided, have led many to conclude that this could not be a man in a suit.

3. Orang-Pendek

Although mysterious hairy bipeds are stereotypically imagined as giant, hulking brutes, there have been reports of exceptions to that rule. The *Orang-Pendek* of the Indonesian island of Sumatra is described as a petite creature standing about 0.75 to 1.5 m tall. Its name means *"little man"* or *"short person."* The creature is said to have a pinkish-brown skin covered by a short, dark fur with a mane of long hair around the face that flows down the back. The Orang-Pendek is sometimes called the *Sedapa,* and in the forests of nearby Borneo there are similar reports of a creature known as the *Batutut.*

Considered more humanlike than apelike, the Orang-Pendek is said to walk mostly upright and to possess relatively short arms. Pint-sized footprints about 15 cm long, shaped very much like human footprints except for being proportionately rather broad, have been presented as evidence of the creature. Some accounts indicate that the Orang-Pendek walks with its feet reversed so that its toes point backward. According to Bigfoot investigator John Napier, this peculiar podiatric condition is a long-recurring theme common to man-monster stories around the world.

Natives of Sumatra have generally accepted the Orang-Pendek as a genuine animal for centuries, and because they believe it to be a gentle creature that only attacks small animals for food, they regard it with tolerance and respect, rather than fear. Sceptics argue that people have mistaken the island's orangutans, gibbons and sun bears as this creature, but Orang-Pendek eyewitnesses insist that what they have seen is none of those animals.

In 1910 there occurred one of the first Orang-Pendek sightings by a European, who reported "a large creature, low on its feet, which ran like a man, and was about to cross my path; it was very hairy and it was not an orangutan; but its face was not like an ordinary man's." A Dutchman named Van Herwaarden reported a similar encounter in 1923. He was an experienced hunter and armed with a rifle, but as would also be the case with Bigfoot spotter William Roe, he found himself unable to shoot the creature because it looked so human. "I suddenly felt that I was going to commit murder," Van Herwaarden said.

Recent years have seen an explosion of interest in the Orang-Pendek, thanks primarily to the efforts of British travel writer Deborah Martyr. During a tour of southwestern Sumatra in 1989, Martyr's guide pointed out areas where Orang-Pendeks were frequently spotted, claiming that he had seen the creature twice himself. This was the first Martyr had ever heard of the Orang-Pendek and she was highly sceptical, but she was intrigued enough to investigate further. Before long, she had the opportunity to examine firsthand the characteristic tiny tracks allegedly made by the creature, and she judged them to be unidentifiable. Martyr was thorough enough to address the most obvious explanation for scaled-down humanlike footprints:

"If we had been reasonably close to a village, I might have momentarily thought the prints to be those of a healthy seven-year-old child," Martyr reported. "The ball of the foot was, however, too broad even for a people who habitually wear no shoes."

Martyr took a plastic cast of the tracks, but unfortunately she sent it to the Indonesian National Parks Department and never saw it again, leaving some to speculate whether the evidence was lost or purposely suppressed. But Martyr continued her search, making a second career out of stalking the Orang-Pendek. In 1994, while on an expedition with an organisation called Flora and Fauna International, Martyr reported making a personal sighting of the creature. She has since claimed to see the Orang-Pendek a total of three times.

4. Chinese Wildman

The *Wildman* has been a part of the folklore of southern and central China for centuries, sighted primarily in the heavily forested areas of these regions. Frequently referred to as the *Yeren* (a Chinese word meaning "wildman"), the creature has been described as about 2 m tall with a thick coat of brown or red hair. It is said to walk upright, and footprints reportedly belonging to the Wildman have measured 40 centimetres.

Although widely considered a superstitious myth in contemporary Chinese society, the Yeren boasts a history of sightings by scientists and dignitaries, rather than just common folk. In 1940, biologist Wang Tselin claimed to examine the corpse of a Wildman that had been killed in the Gansu region. He said it was a female specimen over 2 m tall, with striking features that appeared to be a cross between ape and human. Geologist Fan Jingquan in 1950 reported seeing Wildmen live and in the flesh, a pair that he construed as mother and son, in the forests of the Shanxi province.

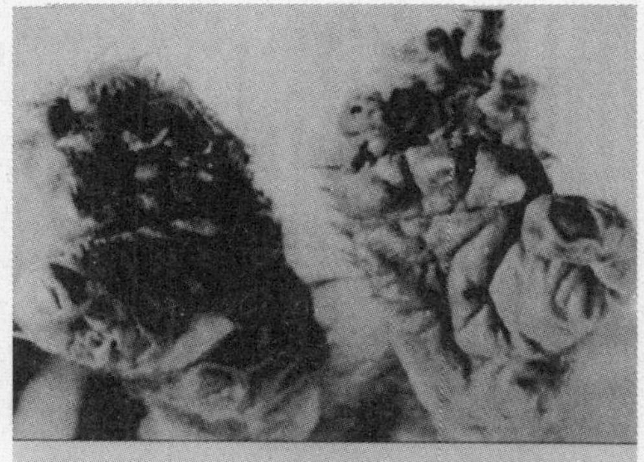

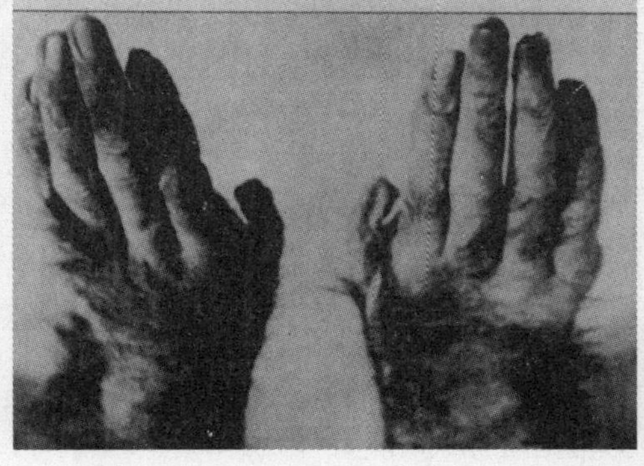

In 1961, a team of road builders allegedly killed a female Yeren in the forests of Xishuang Banna. By the time officials from the Chinese Academy of Sciences made it to the scene, the body had disappeared. The scientists' investigation concluded that the creature, which was described as only one and quarter metre tall, had been an ordinary gibbon. But twenty years later, a journalist who had been involved in the investigation came forward to claim that the creature killed was no gibbon, but an "unknown animal of human shape."

In 1976, a car carrying six local government bureaucrats came across an unidentified creature on a rural highway in the Hubei province. The purported Wildman attempted to flee by climbing up an embankment, but slipped and fell onto the road in front of the car, crouching on all fours in the glare of the headlights. One of the frightened passengers threw a rock at the beast and caused it to run away. This incident sparked another intensive Wildman investigation by the Chinese Academy of Sciences, but it turned up no conclusive results.

The closest thing to concrete proof of the Yeren's existence surfaced in 1980 in the form of the preserved hands and feet of an unknown hominid creature. Supposedly, villagers had killed a Wildman in the Zhejiang province in 1957, and a biology teacher had removed and preserved all four of its extremities. Upon examining the hands and feet, researcher Zhou Guoxing at first announced that they belonged to an unknown species of monkey, but later decided they had come from a large macaque monkey. But Zhou made clear that this discovery did not mean that all Wildmen are macaques.

Another monkey species that has been suggested as a candidate for Wildman sightings is the rare and endangered golden monkey, whose unusual appearance could seem like a man-monster to some observers. Other researchers propose the more unlikely hypothesis that the Yeren is a surviving *Gigantopithecus,* a giant extinct primate believed to have lived in China three hundred thousand years ago.

5. Yowie

Its profound geographical isolation makes Australia an unlikely habitat for a missing link that could exist for millions of years without being documented by science, especially since no primates are indigenous to the continent. Nevertheless, the land down under claims its own version of Bigfoot, the *Yowie,* which has been reported primarily in New South Wales and the Gold Coast of Queensland. The creature's long history can be traced back to aborigine legends.

The earlier name for the creature was the *Yahoo,* which according to some accounts was an aborigine term meaning *"devil"* or *"evil spirit."* But more likely, the indirect source of the name was Jonathan Swift, whose Gulliver's Travels (1726) includes a subhuman race called the Yahoos. Hearing the aborigines's fearful accounts of this malevolent beast, nineteenth-century European settlers probably applied the name Yahoo to the Australian creature themselves.

The first recorded sighting of a Yahoo by a European came in 1881, when an Australian newspaper reported that several witnesses had seen a large baboonlike animal that stood taller than a man. In 1894, another individual claimed to come face to face with a "wild man or gorilla" in New South Wales bush. A 1903 newspaper printed the testimony of a man who said he watched as aborigines killed a Yahoo, which he said looked "like a black man, but covered all over with grey hair."

In 1912, George Summerell was riding on horseback between Bombala and Bemboka when he saw a strange creature on all fours drinking from a creek. The animal rose up on its hind feet to a height of 2 m and looked at Summerell.

Then it disregarded the horseman, finished its drink, and peacefully walked away into nearby woods. The following day, Summerell's friend Sydney Wheeler Jephcott rushed to the scene of the sighting and discovered an abundance of handprints and footprints. Jephcott described the footprints as humanlike but huge, and having only four toes per foot. He said he made plaster casts of the tracks and turned them in to a local university, but there is no record of a scientific analysis being rendered.

Sometime in the 1970s, the term "Yowie" supplanted "Yahoo," for reasons that remain as mysterious as the creature. One possible origin of the newer name is the aborigine word *youree,* described as a legitimate native term for the hairy man-monster. The Australian accent could easily contort "youree" into "Yowie."

In 1971, a Royal Australian Air Force helicopter carrying a crew of surveyors landed atop Sentinel Mountain, a remote and inaccessible peak. Much to their surprise, the team discovered fresh footprints in mud, much larger than human footprints, in a place where no known biped could possibly be present.

Yowie sightings continued steadily throughout the '70s. In 1976, backpackers in New South Wales reported seeing a 1.5 m female Yowie whose fur stank to high heaven. Also in New South Wales, Betty Gee reported seeing a giant creature covered with black fur outside her home in 1977. Shortly thereafter, her fence was knocked down and large footprints surrounded the scene. A man in the Gold Coast city of Springbrook said that a "big black hairy man-thing" appeared before him while he was chopping wood in 1978. "It just stared at me and I stared back," he said. "I was so numb, I couldn't even raise the axe I had in my hand."

In 1997, a woman residing in Tanimi Desert was awakened at 3 am by a horrible animal-like noise just outside her bedroom window. When she went out to investigate, she was confronted with an unbearable stench that sent her into the dry heaves, and she saw a 2 m hairy creature tear through her fence as it made a hasty retreat. The next day, police discovered a number of giant footprints and a somewhat shredded irrigation pipe that had seemingly been chewed upon. Some Yowie theorists speculated that a current drought had forced the creatures into inhabited areas to find water.

The Yowie may be nothing but a tall tale, and it may be rooted in a fanciful ancient legend. An aborigine folk tale explains that when their people first migrated to Australia thousands of years ago, they encountered on the new continent a savage race of ape-men. The aborigines's ancestors went to war against the ape-men, and in the end the humans triumphed, thanks to their ability to make weapons. Some have wondered if this tale might contain some element of truth, and it is a few diehard survivors from this unknown primate species that would later be known as the Yahoo and the Yowie.

6. Skunk Ape

Other mysterious primates of the world may be more famous, and more fearsome, and more celebrated in tantalisingly indistinct frames of 16mm film, but only one big hairy monster can rightfully claim to be the stinkiest: the *Skunk Ape* of the Florida Everglades.

The creature is generally described as being about 2 m tall and 140 kg, covered in a dark fur the colour of mud, and bearing a distinct and far-ranging aroma redolent of an unholy mixture of skunk, rotten eggs and cow manure. "It stank awful, like a dog that hasn't been bathed in a year and suddenly gets rained on," Charlie Stoeckman said in an evocative account of his Skunk Ape sighting in the Florida Keys in 1977.

Some accounts indicate that the Skunk Ape has been a part of Everglades lore for decades, but the swamp beast only became widely reported in the cultural aftermath of the 1967 Patterson Bigfoot film. In addition to being an era of Bigfoot mania, the 1970s were also the period when developers began a concerted foray into the Everglades. This led to large numbers of out-of-towners being exposed to the colourful legends of the local folk, who may have been willing to spin extravagant tall tales of the Skunk Ape just to fool the city slickers.

Early stories of the Skunk Ape contained a conspiratorial edge, as it was rumoured that the government had captured a living specimen and the Army held it captive in a secret vault at Everglades National Park, until the Skunk Ape smashed through a concrete wall and escaped. There are dozens of sightings on record from throughout the '70s, almost all of them containing a specification of the creature's pungent odour.

And on the whole, the tales are more tongue-in-cheek than most monster sightings usually are — the Skunk Ape is regarded as an old buddy rather than a terror of the wild, and in some cases, you can almost see the eyewitness winking at you in the words of his report.

"Sometimes, sitting by the fire, I'd hear him walking in the brush," Jim Spink said in describing a Skunk Ape encounter from 1975. "He'd approach, standing there in the jungle. I knew he was there. I'd say, 'Hi, come on in. Have some coffee.' But he never did."

Although Skunk Ape sightings have slacked off in recent years, the creature enjoyed something of a comeback in 1997. A guided tour group in Ochopee saw a large, apelike animal ambling through the outskirts of a swamp. Soon afterwards, Ochopee fire chief Vince Doerr saw a similar creature cross the road near his home and rush into the swamp. Doerr managed to take a distant snapshot of the supposed Skunk Ape before it disappeared.

7. Piltdown Man

The story of the *Piltdown Man* is a cautionary tale for those who think it's only the uneducated trailer-park masses who can be duped into believing faulty evidence of an uncovered missing link — the scientific community at large can be fooled just as well. This infamous hoax dates back to 1910, when labourers at a gravel pit in the English village of Piltdown unearthed a peculiar fossil they thought looked like a shard of coconut. They brought it to Charles Dawson, an attorney who was the steward of the property, and also an amateur archaeologist.

Dawson was thrilled with the artifact, which he thought might be a skull fragment of extreme antiquity. He gradually accumulated further pieces of bone from the gravel pit, and in 1912, he presented his findings to Arthur Smith Woodward, a geologist at the Natural History Museum in London. Soon afterwards, Smith Woodward led a thorough examination of the gravel pit, promptly discovering more skull fragments and a piece of jawbone.

The skull bones seemed human, yet the jawbone was apelike. Given the proximity of the pieces and their uniform colour, Smith Woodward declared them to have belonged to a single individual, a primitive species belonging to the undocumented transition between ape and human. The bones supported the theory that early man would have developed a larger brain before evolving a humanlike jaw.

The news of Piltdown Man took the world by storm, but not everyone was willing to accept the existence of this proposed "earliest Englishman." The foremost objection was the unlikelihood of this skull and this jawbone fitting together in some unprecedented mishmash of a primate. But no one could conclusively disprove it, so for years Piltdown Man sat unmovable as a stumbling block that contradicted the rest of paleontology.

In 1953, Oxford anatomist Joseph Weiner argued that Piltdown Man possessed a jawbone from an ape that had been deliberately stained and altered. After a series of tests using new dating techniques, it was discovered that all of the Piltdown bones were less than a thousand years old, and that the jawbone had been chemically treated to appear much older. Later tests would prove that the jaw had come from an orangutan. The Piltdown Man was a complete hoax.

The only question remaining, though, was whodunit. For nearly fifty years, the identity of the guilty party remained a complete and baffling enigma. Most people believed that Dawson was in on the scam, but he was too inexperienced an authority to have created the faked fossils alone. It appeared that the Piltdown prank was destined to be a mystery for the ages.

But in 1996, a canvas trunk was discovered stashed away at the Natural History Museum, and it contained a number of fossils stained in the same manner as the Piltdown bones. The trunk bore the initials of Martin Hinton, a zoologist and fossil expert at the Museum, who was known for his love of practical jokes.

Authorities now agree that Hinton was the mastermind behind Piltdown Man, and the bones found in his trunk were practice runs at the big prank. Hinton would have been motivated by a desire to humiliate Smith Woodward, whom Hinton considered pompous and arrogant, especially after refusing to support funding for a research project Hinton once proposed. You might say that Hinton's only failure was that his hoax was too good, since Smith Woodward died several years before the embarrassing truth about his "scientific breakthrough" was revealed.

8. De Loys's Ape

In 1920, Swiss geologist Francois de Loys was on an expedition in the jungles of Venezuela and Colombia when his group was ambushed by a pair of threatening animals that appeared to be apes. De Loys' men shot the creatures, and marvelling at the strange appearance of these primates, they decided to take a photograph. The crew sat one of the *ape* corpses on a crate and propped it up with a stick under its chin, and the resulting photo is one of the most infamous images in the realm of cryptozoology — considered at one time possible evidence of a genuine missing link that had actually been captured and documented.

De Loys filed away the photograph with his notes on the expedition and it went unnoticed for years, reportedly because the geologist didn't think the animal was anything more significant than a mild curiosity. His friend George Montandon, a Swiss anthropologist, accidentally discovered the photo in 1929 while looking through de Loys's records. Montandon believed that it depicted an undiscovered species of ape, and that de Loys had unwittingly made an important scientific find.

De Loys and Montandon brought the story and the photograph to the attention of the press and the scientific establishment, arguing that this animal was a previously unknown ancestor of mankind. Sceptics debated de Loys's estimate of the animal's height having been 1.6 m, which was 45 cm taller than the largest monkeys in the Americas. But careful analysis of scale in the photograph, based on the known dimensions of the type of fuel crate the dead animal had been seated upon, indicated that de Loys was correct in judging its size. Expeditions ventured to South America in hopes of finding further specimens, but came back empty-handed.

And so it was accepted, with varying degrees of certainty, that de Loys had documented a new and rare breed of ape, which Montandon had named *Ameranthropoides loysi,* in honour of its discoverer. This belief persisted for years, until authorities such as Bernard Heuvelmans, Ivan T. Sanderson and others revisited the de Loys photograph and decided that this creature was no mystery ape, but a large spider monkey. The specimen shown is admittedly abnormally big for a spider monkey, and it may be an unidentified variety of that species, but the notion that it might be an ape and some sort of missing link is definitely baloney.

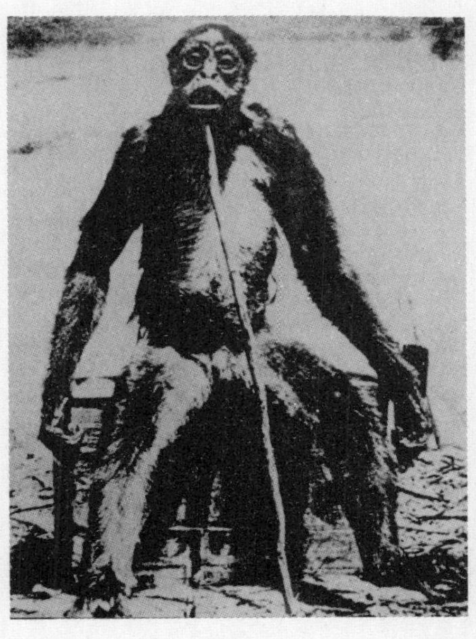

As a bizarre postscript to this story, cryptozoologists Loren Coleman and Michel Raynal announced their findings in 1996 that the de Loys photo may have been a tool in a racist pseudoscience agenda on the part of Montandon. It was previously not widely known that Montandon's scientific views were coloured by white Aryan supremacy ideology, such as his recommendation in the late 1930s that Jewish women should have their noses cut off to render them less attractive as potential breeders.

Montandon subscribed to a crackpot evolution theory called *"polygenism,"* which held that the various human races had evolved independently from different species of ape, thus rationalising the superiority of one race over another. Montandon seized upon the de Loys photo as a possible way to fill in a missing piece of the polygenism puzzle, because the theory had lacked an American ape that could have evolved into the Native American race. Few of those who supported the *"de Loys' ape"* hypothesis over the years could possibly have known they were indirectly lending credence to a fallacious and evil-minded theory.

9. Minnesota Iceman

In 1968, the year after Roger Patterson captured the world's imagination with his notorious Bigfoot film, Minnesota carnival huckster Frank Hansen began travelling the American sideshow circuit to exhibit a startling attraction: *"The Famous Missing Link Iceman."* This was the alleged corpse of a 2 m, hairy man-monster, which lay frozen solid in a coffin of ice. Hansen did a brisk business at thirty-five cents a peek!

Hansen told varying tales of where the Iceman came from, but the gist of his story was that a crew of either Russian or Japanese fishermen had discovered the body off the coast of Siberia, frozen in a giant block of ice. From there, the creature made its way to an emporium in Hong Kong, where it was purchased by an anonymous American oil millionaire. For whatever reason, this eccentric tycoon then rented his extravagant purchase to Hansen, so that it might be displayed before the carnival-going masses. A far-fetched tale to be sure, but hang on — it gets even worse.

In a *Fortean Times* interview in 1995, Hansen indicated that he was terrified of going on the road with the Iceman because it was so extraordinarily valuable. The liability he would face in the event of an accident was too much for Hansen to risk. And so, he says, he took the frozen corpse to "some friends in the movie industry" in California, and asked them to create a replica of the creature.

A few months later, these friends had produced a satisfactory duplicate, and Hansen says it is this replica — and never the original — that he put on public display.

Hansen's first tour with the Iceman was a sensational success. The only snag that came up was when US customs detained him after a one-day excursion into Canada. Customs was concerned that Hansen might be illegally transporting a cadaver, or that the body might pose a health hazard. Indignant, Hansen called up his senator, Walter Mondale, and the future Vice President was kind enough to pull the right strings to let the Iceman come back home.

News of the Iceman grabbed the attention of two prominent cryptozoologists, Ivan T. Sanderson and Bernard Heuvelmans. Sanderson called Hansen and asked for permission to visit his home in Minnesota and view the creature. Hansen says that he turned down Sanderson's request, but a few days later, Sanderson turned up at Hansen's doorstep, along with his Belgian colleague Heuvelmans. Hansen recalls that he initially refused to show the men the creature, but after the three of them shared a quart of gin, he relented.

It is unclear whether the Iceman that Sanderson and Heuvelmans saw was the "original" corpse or Hansen's "fabricated illusion," but in either case, the two experts were stunned. They agreed that this was an actual animal, a specimen of an unknown primate species. They took photographs and made elaborate sketches, although the opacity of the ice keep them from observing as much detail as they would have liked. Hansen flatly refused their request to open the lid, but Heuvelmans later shattered the glass cover accidentally by dropping a light bulb on it. A horrible stench escaped from within, alarming

Sanderson because the smell of putrefication meant that the body must be rapidly decomposing, and needed to be thoroughly examined by scientists before any further deterioration.

Following Sanderson and Heuvelmans's visit, the Smithsonian Institution contacted Hansen and asked to examine the Iceman. At this point, he announced that the original specimen had been returned to its millionaire owner, and he was now touring with a replica. Beginning to smell a rat, the Smithsonian soon dropped its interest in the case, but Hansen next attracted the attention of the FBI. Heuvelmans had noted an apparent bullet wound in one eye of the Iceman, and he suspected for some reason that it might have been killed in Vietnam. The FBI briefly considered the possibility of foul play, but declined to pursue the matter officially. Nonetheless, Hansen capitalised on a half-truth by promoting his star attraction as "investigated by the FBI."

Embarrassed by their compulsive gullibility, Sanderson and Heuvelmans backed away from their initial endorsement of the Iceman. Sanderson investigated Hansen's claims of having the creature duplicated by movie prop artists, and discovered that three Californian companies had manufactured latex Icemen for Hansen as early as 1967.

The most logical scenario is that there was no millionaire owner and no real monster, and Hansen changed the story about his fake creation whenever reality began to pry too deeply. First he introduced the story of the "replica switcheroo" after Sanderson and Heuvelmans brought scientists breathing down his neck, and then he retroactively stretched the substitution tale back to before the Iceman's first tour, once word was out that he'd had Hollywood build props for him since the beginning.

Such duplicity should hardly be surprising from a sideshow con-man. Just to top all his other lies, Hansen began saying in his later years that the bullet wound in the creature's eye was where he had shot it while hunting in Minnesota, throwing his whole elaborate Iceman mythology out of the window.

10. Oliver the Mutant Chimp

A chimpanzee named *Oliver* stumped and astonished scientists for nearly twenty years. He is physiologically unusual, with a lack of hair on his chest and head, and a jawline and ears that are shaped differently from normal chimps. But more notably, Oliver very much acts human. Way too human.

Oliver was born in the Congo and sold to South African animal trainers Frank and Janet Burger in the early 1970s. From his youth he seemed not to belong with the other chimps, preferring instead to socialise with humans. He always walked upright and learned to use the toilet. His owners found that he enjoyed chores such as pushing a wheelbarrow and preparing dog food for the family dogs. Oliver was also fond of relaxing by watching television and drinking Seven-Up and whiskey. When his mind turned to sexual thoughts, Oliver was not interested in female chimps — he went after Mrs. Burger and any other human women he saw.

Oliver's libido eventually forced the Burgers to sell him to an American trainer, and Oliver began a career of travelling as a trained chimp, demonstrating all manner of highly intelligent behaviour. He came to be promoted as *"The Missing Link,"* and there was much speculation about his genetic makeup. It was widely rumoured that Oliver was a mutant chimp or even a human-chimp hybrid, perhaps the result of some secret genetic experiment. Some news reports indicated that Oliver had 47 chromosomes, one less than a chimpanzee, one more than a human.

In 1997, a series of genetic tests finally settled the question of what exactly Oliver is made of. Geneticists at the University of Chicago determined that Oliver is simply a chimp, not a missing link, and certainly no human-chimp hybrid. He also possesses the standard chimpanzee chromosome count of 48.

"So the report of 47 chromosomes was either a misinterpretation or purposeful misrepresentation," said Dr. David Ledbetter, who performed the analysis and found to his surprise that the results matched tests done two decades earlier. "The chimp-human question was settled twenty years ago," he said.

Scientists plan further tests to search for a genetic explanation of Oliver's unusual appearance and behaviour. Other upright-walking chimps have appeared elsewhere, suggesting that Oliver might be part of a new species. In the meantime, the middle-aged chimp has retired to a Texas sanctuary called 'Primarily Primates', where he has happily settled down with a female chimp, having finally accepted that human ladies must be out of his league.

11. Almas

Almas, also known as *Almasty* and *Albasty* are strange apelike creatures allegedly resembling the Neanderthal man that reportedly live in the Caucasus Mountains, in the republic of Kazakhstan, central Asia.

In the Caucasus, Almas (which in the Mongolian language means *'wildman'*) are well known by the local people, who tell numerous stories of an apparent familiarity between humans and these creatures. Eyewitness accounts dating back hundreds of years describe Almas communicating with humans by means of gestures. There were even stories of Almas bartering food for trinkets.

Adult Almases have been described as being at least 1.5 m tall, shy, hairy, with prominent eyebrow ridges, a receding chin and a jaw that protrudes out.

Other names by which these creatures are known, depending on the particular region, are *'Wind-Man', Abnuaaya, Bekk-Bok, Biabin-Guli, Gul-Biavan, Guli-Avan, Golub-Yavan, Kaptar, Kra-Dhan, Ksy-Giik or Ksy Gyik, Mirygdy, Mulen* and *Voita.*

Almas Timeline:

1420 — The first known printed reference on the Almas was made by a Bavarian named Hans Schiltberger. He travelled through the Tien Shan mountains as a captive to the Mongols. During his imprisonment he kept a journal in which he wrote:

"In the mountains themselves live a wild people, who have nothing in common with other human beings, a pelt covers the entire body of these creatures. Only the hands and face are free of hair. They run around in the hills like animals and eat foliage and grass and whatever else they can find. The Lord of the Territory made Egidi a present of a couple of forest people, a man and a woman, together with three untamed horses the sizes of asses and all sorts of other animals which are not found in German lands and which I cannot therefore put a name to."

1807-1867 — Sightings reported at Khalkha, the Galbin Gobi and Dzakh Soudjin Gobi as well as in Inner Mongolia;

also at the Gourban Bogdin Gobi, Chardzyn Gobi and the Alachan desert.

Mid 1800s — A wild reddish-black hair covered woman with both Mongoloid and Negroid features, dark skin, broad body, large hands and feet and a sloped forehead, was allegedly captured in the western Caucasus region of Abkhazia, and given the name Zana or Zanya. According to accounts, she was physically very powerful, able to perform feats of exceptional strength.

While in captivity, Zana was passed on through a succession of owners, including noblemen, and mothered several children (she was reputed to have a fondness for wine, which supposedly played a role in her pregnancies). According to the story, she had as many as six offspring, by different men. Of these, the first two perished, due to Zana washing them in cold water after birth. The other four survived with the help of the local village women, who took care of the children. They were fairly normal, except for being dark and physically powerful, and grew up accepted among the villagers. Each of these children reproduced and allegedly had descendants throughout the region, up to nowadays. Zana died sometime in the 1880s.

1881 — As almost to confirm Hans Schiltberger's journal, a Russian named Nicholai Przewalski rediscovered the horses the sizes of asses and called them, of course, the *"Przewalski horses";* he also reported seeing 'wildmen' in Mongolia in 1871.

1906 — Badzare Baradyine, while on a caravan at the desert of Alachan, reports seeing a "hairy man standing on the top of a sand dune, outlined against the sunset." After being approached by the Imperial Russian Geographical Society's president and asked not to publish the incident, Badzare complies, but relays the information about his sighting to a personal friend, Mongolian professor Tsyben Zhamtsarano, who in turn begins a lengthy and determined investigation of the Almas.

1907-1940 — Professor Tsyben Zhamtsarano compiles eyewitness's accounts and recruits an artist to draw the likeness of the Almas based on the gathered descriptions. He also plots sightings locations and dates on a map of the region. After being imprisoned in Russia for a number of years, the professor dies in 1940. His files vanish and are rumoured to be confiscated by the authorities.

1937 — Dordji Meiren, an associate of Professor Zhamtsarano, reports seeing a carpet made out of a hide of an Almas, being used by lamas in ritual ceremonies at their monastery.

1941 — A Russian unit fighting the Germans in the Caucasus near Buinakst is asked by some partisans to look at an unusual prisoner. According to the unit's commander, Lt. Col. Vargen Karapetyan, the captive *'man'* was naked, hairy, and covered with lice; he obviously didn't understand speech and appeared to be dim-witted, blinking often; he was evidently afraid, but made no attempt to defend himself when Karapetyan pulled hairs from his body. He was kept in a barn, because, as the partisans explained, in a heated room he stank and dripped sweat. Not wanting to get involved, Karapetyan told the partisans to do what they wanted with the prisoner. A few days later he heard that the prisoner had escaped, but according to a later report made by the Ministry of the Interior in Daghestan, the 'wild man' had been executed as a deserter after being court-martialled.

1963 — Ivan Ivlov, a Russian paediatrician, sees a family of manlike creatures consisting of a male, female and a small child, standing on a mountain slope. Ivlov observed the creatures through field glasses for some time before they vanished behind a jutting rock. Ivlov's Mongol driver also sees the creatures and assures him they are common in the area.

1964 — Russian historian Boris Porshnev visits the place where Zana had reportedly lived. Several centenarians (Caucasus people are noted for their longevity) claimed to have known her and to have attended her funeral. Dr. Porshnev also meets a couple of the alleged descendants (her grandchildren) of the wild woman, and wrote of the episode:

"From the moment I saw Zana's grandchildren, I was impressed by their dark skin and Negroid looks. Shalikula, the grandson, has unusually powerful jaw muscles, and he can pick up a chair, with a man sitting on it, with his teeth."

During the next few years, Porshnev and a colleague tried to find Zana's remains in the Genaba (the family name of her descendants) graveyard, and although they found the vaguely Neanderthaloid bones of what they speculated was one of her children, they never discovered the remnants of the Almas herself.

1972 — An unnamed Russian doctor met a family of Almas, according to British anthropologist Myra Shackley, who adds that their "very simple lifestyle and the nature of their appearance suggests strongly that Almas might represent the survival of a prehistoric way of life, and perhaps even of an earlier form of man. The best candidate is undoubtedly the Neanderthal man."

1985 — Maya Bykova, an assistant to Dr. Boris Porshnev (yes, the same one from 1964) at Moscow's Darwin Museum, is reported to have actually observed a hominoid of unknown identity, a creature nicknamed by the ethnic Mnasi people as *Mecheny,* or *"marked,"* because of the whitish skin patch seen on its left forearm, the only part of its body not covered by red-brown hair.

12. Nessie

The *Loch Ness* Monster is obviously the most famous aquatic mystery animal in the world, and she is rivalled only by Bigfoot as the best known cryptozoological entity of all time. Beyond that, it's hard to get anyone to agree on much of anything about *Nessie.* The date of the earliest sighting of strangeness at Loch Ness is a matter of much dispute. Some claim that Nessie has been around as far back as medieval times, citing a traditional tale of St. Columba repelling a monster in the adjoining River Ness in 565 A.D., by invoking the name of God. But most evidence indicates that the Loch Ness Monster did not appear until 1933, at least not as we know her. It seems that overzealous Nessie historians have looked back through the centuries and retroactively linked a disparate array of strange Loch Ness occurrences and sightings to the monster's legend, even if there is no connection beyond geography.

The encounter most accepted as the first modern Nessie sighting took place in April 1933, as Mr. and Mrs. John Mackay drove along the north shore of Loch Ness. Mrs. Mackay noticed a flurry of movement in the lake about 100 m from the shore. She initially thought the disturbance was two ducks fighting, but then the couple saw two dark humps cutting across the water. Mrs. Mackay estimated the combined length of the humps at about 6 m. The creature, which the observers described as an "enormous animal rolling and plunging," quickly submerged just before reaching the opposite shore.

A local newspaper, the *Inverness Courier*, ran a report on the sighting in its May 2 edition, in which editor Evan Barron proclaimed the unknown animal a "monster." The story reached great popularity across Scotland. Coincidentally, at that time a road running beside Loch Ness was expanded and a large amount of surrounding foliage was cleared away, in effect opening up the lake to far more visibility around much of its perimeter. This provided richer opportunities for the curious monster-watchers that came from all around, and by October of that year, there were over 20 additional sightings of the lake creature on record. Some of them — if not all — were assuredly copycat fabrications aimed at getting in on the latest fad. But the Loch Ness Monster was here to stay.

Among the most peculiar reports from that silly season of 1933, Mr. and Mrs. George Spicer claimed that they were driving up the lake's eastern shore on July 22 when they saw a huge, long-necked creature lying in the road ahead of them — a rare land sighting of Nessie. The Spicers say their car nearly crashed into the monster, which was about 8-10 m long, but the beast then crawled ponderously into the underbrush and presumably dived back into its watery home.

The first supposed photograph of Nessie was taken by Hugh Gray in November 1933. It shows what might be considered a blurry appendage of some sort, perhaps a long neck or a flipper, extending from the water. But Gray's photo is almost certainly a golden retriever or Labrador swimming with a large stick in its mouth.

Far more famous is a picture taken in April 1934 by Dr. Robert Kenneth Wilson, which has long been considered the classic Loch Ness Monster photo. Widely known as "the surgeon's photograph" (even though Wilson was actually a gynaecologist), it clearly depicts the archetypal sloping neck and small, reptilian head most people imagine when they think of Nessie. But in 1994 — the 60th anniversary of the surgeon's photo — it was revealed that the photo was a hoax, created by fastening a neck and head of wood and plastic onto a toy submarine.

Some of the most convincing evidence of the Loch Ness Monster was collected in August 1972, when a group of scientific investigators collected an extraordinary series of underwater photographs. The MIT Academy of Applied Sciences joined forces with the Loch Ness Investigation Bureau to conduct a thorough scanning of the lake. The team, led by the Academy's Robert Rines, used a sonar device equipped with a camera set to take pictures automatically when the sonar detected any large objects in its path.

In the early morning hours of August 8, the sonar picked up two large objects about 6-9 m long, indicated that schools of salmon were fleeing in front of them. The signals lasted only a matter of minutes.

When the underwater photos were developed, two of them showed what appeared to be close-ups of a large, diamond-shaped fin. A third showed a far more dramatic image: an apparent full-body shot of Nessie, fitting the classical description of a long neck, thick body and stubby flippers. The Academy team hit pay dirt again in July 1975, with a further series of underwater pictures which seemed to show Nessie's body and close-ups of her head.

With the combination of repeated sonar and photographic evidence, it was beginning to seem that proof of the Loch Ness Monster might finally be at hand. Mainstream establishments such as the Smithsonian Institution, Harvard University and *Time* magazine expressed willingness to accept that the creature might be real.

Then in 1984, *Discover* magazine published an exposé charging Robert Rines with retouching and altering the photos when he had used computer enhancements at Jet Propulsion Laboratory to "clarify" the images before releasing them for review. JPL officials and members of the Academy team dismissed these accusations, asserting that nothing false had been added during the enhancement process. Other critics have noted that the head in the 1975 pictures looks like a tree stump or an engine block — two sorts of objects fully proven to exist in Loch Ness.

Sceptics from London's Natural History Museum pointed out that in the 1972 photo supposedly showing the creature's body, it seems apparent that the "head" is not connected to the "neck." The gap may only be a shadowy spot, but as you can see here for yourself, it's likely the head is a separate object that seems like a continuous anatomical feature only by virtue of its random placement, and our willingness to believe.

Some of the most famous Nessie photos of recent years were taken in May 1977 by Tony Shiels, an eccentric psychic entertainer better known as "Doc" Shiels. He made a side career of hunting sea monsters, and in 1976 Shiels had garnered attention for stalking and photographing *Morgawr,* the Cornish beast of Falmouth Bay. In the following year, he set his sights on the biggest catch of them all.

After camping out lakeside at Urquhart Castle for three days, Shiels claims he saw the humps of the creature cutting across the morning waters. Several other eyewitnesses were reportedly on hand. Later that afternoon, Shiels apparently caught Nessie sticking her head out of the water to have a look around, and snapped two photographs.

"The part of the neck showing above the water-line must have been around 1.2 or 1.5 m long," Shiels said. "The colour of the animal was greenish brown, with a paler underside, skin texture smooth and glossy. The animal was visible for no more than 4 or 5 seconds. It held itself very upright, very still, except for a turning of the head and a straightening of the neck before it sank very smoothly, below the surface. It had powerful neck muscles."

Shiels's photos have been reproduced thousands of times as illustrations for Loch Ness sightings, threatening to overtake the "Surgeon's Photograph" as the definitive image of Nessie. But experts have almost universally dismissed them as fakes.

Aside from the all-too-perfect appearance of the monster in the Shiels pictures, one must consider the dubious background of the man behind the lens. As a professional showman and self-described wizard, Shiels has earned a living by performing outrageous, pseudo-mystical stunts. In addition to Nessie and Morgawr, he has photographed sea monsters from at least half a dozen sites around Great Britain, which seems awfully convenient.

Doc Shiels himself has reportedly shown an affidavit to his photos authenticity, and yet some of his ambiguous commentary on the matter suggests that he finds the whole thing absurd and deeply amusing. He supposedly once remarked that he most definitely took the photos, but he does not believe in them (whatever *that* means).

Putting aside all the ups and downs of the wealth of Nessie evidence, is it in any way possible that the creature might be real? Maybe, but it's doubtful that she exists in the form popularly imagined. The prevalent conception of Nessie as a long-necked, flipper amphibian is a close match for the actual prehistoric beast known as the *plesiosaur.* But in addition to being extinct, plesiosaurs breathed air and lived on land and they were way too big to possibly survive in Loch Ness. Ecological studies in 1993 proved that the lake's fish population is far too small to support a predator of over 300 kg, ruling out an animal of the size commonly attributed to Nessie.

The current opinion among experts is that a large number of Nessie sightings can be attributed to the Baltic sturgeon. A large fish that grows up to 3 m long with a prominent dorsal fin towards its back, the sturgeon has a narrow, reptile-like snout that could pierce the surface and look a lot like the sloping neck of a sea monster.

13. Champ

The notorious sea beast of Lake Champlain, a 175 km long lake on the border of New York and Vermont, is considered America's Loch Ness Monster. Popular legend has it that the French explorer Samuel de Champlain saw the creature in 1609, in the first ever sighting of a North American lake monster. But this apocryphal tale has been traced back to a mistaken account made by a reporter in 1960. It seems that Champlain did, in fact, spot a strange aquatic monster, but the location was off the coast of the St. Lawrence estuary, and not the lake that bears the explorer's name.

Probably the earliest known report of a monster in Lake Champlain came from pioneer settlers near Port Henry, NY, in 1819. A railroad crew near Dresden, NY, in 1873 claimed to see "a head of an enormous serpent sticking out of the water and approaching them from the opposite shore." Following that sighting, area farmers reported missing livestock, along with supposed drag marks stretching across the ground to the shore of the lake. That same year, P. T. Barnum offered a $50,000 reward for any monster hunter who could bring him the "hide of the great Champlain serpent to add to my mammoth World's Fair Show."

Barnum had no takers, but the sightings continued. In 1883, Clinton County Sheriff Nathan Mooney said he saw "an enormous snake or water serpent, 7.5 to 9 metres in length," which raised its long, curved neck about one and half m out of the water. A group of fishermen in 1899 claimed to witness the creature partially climbing onto the shore, exposing about 2 m of its finned body. In 1945, a man claimed to have caught a 35 cm "baby sea serpent" at the lake, but it is thought to have been a salamander.

The most famous sighting of *Champ* in recent times was made in July 1977 by Sandra Mansi, who was vacationing in Vermont near the Canadian border. When she and her husband saw what appeared to be the head and long neck of a huge creature, she managed to grab a camera and take one picture before it vanished. Expert analysis of the Mansi photograph has concluded that the image was not faked or retouched, and it has been widely speculated that the animal shown is a plesiosaur, the same prehistoric species often proposed as Nessie's true identity. Along more realistic lines, some suggest that the apparent head and neck might actually be the fin of a small whale rolling on its side. The credibility of the photo has also been hindered by Mansi's inability to indicate the area from which she took the picture.

Former teacher Joseph W. Zarzynski is the founder of the Lake Champlain Phenomenon Investigation, and the leading authority on Champ for the past twenty years. Zarzynski, who says there has been a total of over 300 Champ sightings, has reported promising results from sonar and electronic surveillance of the lake, but nothing conclusive yet. He is so certain of the creature's reality that he has convinced local and state governments to grant Champ some select measures as a legally protected species.

If there really are sea monsters living anywhere in the United States, Lake Champlain is about as ideal a habitat as anyone could ask for. It is vast in size, surpassed only by the Great Lakes, with depths of up to 120 metres. Champlain contains the populations of fish and aquatic life that would be necessary to sustain a colony of giant beasts, and with its outlet to the Atlantic, it could be home to a much wider diversity of unknown life than a small, isolated lake such as the Loch Ness.

14. Morgawr

The most famous sea beast native to England is *Morgawr,* a creature thought to live in Cornwall's Falmouth Bay. Although Morgawr means *"sea giant"* in the ancient Cornish language, the creature does not possess much of an ancient history. Sightings of Morgawr seem to have started only since the 1970s.

In September 1975, two people reported seeing a massive creature with a humped back, a long, bristled neck, and a head topped with stumpy horns. They said it dived beneath the surface and then reappeared with an eel hanging from its mouth.

A woman known only as "Mary F." claimed to have sighted Morgawr in February 1976, and she was able to take two photographs. She submitted the photos anonymously to the local newspaper, the *Falmouth Packet,* which published them on its front page on March 5, 1976. Mary F. included a note containing the description of what she had seen.

"It looked like an elephant waving its trunk, but the trunk was a long neck with a small head on the end, like a snake's head. It had humps on the back which moved in a funny way. The colour was black or very dark brown, and the skin seemed to be like a sea lion's... the animal frightened me. I would not like to see it any closer. I do not like the way it moved when swimming."

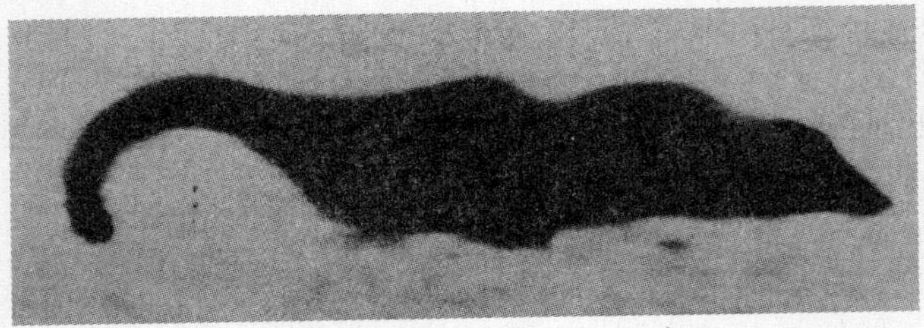

She also indicated that the creature was about 4.5 to 5.4 m long, and that it was visible only for a few seconds. She apologised for the poor quality of her photography, writing that "The pictures are not very clear because of the sun shining right into the camera and a haze on the water. Also, I took them very quickly indeed."

Still, her pictures and her description are among the more feasible evidence of lake monsters on record, and certainly the most substantive sighting of Morgawr. Professional psychic entertainer Tony "Doc" Shiels, who was living near Cornwall, photographed Morgawr in July 1976. Considering his background as a showman, and the fact that Shiels was also lucky enough to photograph Nessie the following year, it seems strongly suspicious that Shiels may have fabricated his photos to cash in on the then-current sensation stirred by the Mary F. photos.

Morgawr has since been sighted periodically, particularly during a rash of reports in 1985, and also by a number of modern-day witches, who have claimed success with pagan "monster-raising" rituals that involve swimming naked in the creature's waters.

15. Morag

Nessie may be the most famous lake monster in Scotland, but she's far from the only one ever reported there. 120 km southwest of Loch Ness, Loch Morar claims to be the home of a beast called *Morag.* The name is derived from the Gaelic Mhorag (pronounced "Vorack"), meaning *"spirit of the lake."*

According to the Loch Morar Survey, a group of biologists devoted to searching for Morag, there have been over thirty credible sightings of the creature that date back to 1887. In the 1930s, during Nessie's first celebrated span of popularity, Morag was frequently reported and generally described as a rapid-moving, hump-backed creature about 9 m in length, with a long neck.

In August 1969, Duncan McDonell and William Simpson were turning their motorboat to the shore of Loch Morar after a day of fishing. Suddenly they found themselves having a close encounter with the legend of the lake, as McDonell later explained:

"I heard a splashing or disturbance in the water astern of us. I looked up and about twenty metres behind us, this creature was coming directly after us in our wake. It took only a matter of seconds to catch up on us. It grazed the side of the boat. I am quite certain this was unintentional. When it struck the boat, it seemed to come to a halt or at least slow down. I grabbed the oar and was attempting to fend it off, my one fear being that if it got under the boat it might capsize it."

In desperation, Simpson grabbed a rifle and fired a shot at the creature, which then slowly sank out of sight. During the five-minute experience, the men said they could clearly see the rough brown skin of the creature's humped back. They estimated it to be about 7.5 - 9 m long, and said that it swam as fast as 50 km/h. McDonell claimed to glimpse the creature's head, which looked like a snake's and was about 30 cm wide.

In April 1971, Ewan Gillies and his son John reported seeing Morag swimming peacefully across the lake as they watched from the shore. They described the creature as about 9 m long, with two or three humps on its back and a small head no thicker than its long, slender neck. The elder Gillies went for a camera and shot two pictures, but the developed film showed nothing unusual.

In fact, there are no significant Morag photos on record, and the only evidence available is eyewitness accounts. In 1996, a mysterious skeleton was dredged up from a depth of 20 m beneath Loch Morar. Analysis revealed that the carcass was not a dead Morag, but the badly deteriorated remains of a deer. Undeterred, the monster-hunting diver who found the bones offered the following shaky hypothesis: "...the only reason that they could have been so deep in the water is if they are the remains of Morag's dinner."

16. Ogopogo

Lake Okanagan in British Columbia, Canada, is said to be the home of a Nessie-like aquatic creature called *Ogopogo.* The origin of the monster's name is itself a matter of some contention. One story has it that *Ogopogo* is a Native American term meaning *"the remorseful one,"* in a reference to an Indian legend of a murderer who was transformed into a hideous serpent as punishment for his crimes. But it turns out that the actual Indian name for the creature is *"N'ha-a-tik,"* and "Ogopogo" is actually derived from a satirical rewriting of an old English dance hall song, which ran in part as follows:

His mother was an earwig,
His father was a whale;
A little bit of head and hardly any tail —
And Ogopogo was his name.

Sightings of Ogopogo run back as far as 1860, when the Lake Okanagan area was first colonised by settlers of European descent. The earliest reports involve objects floating across the water that at first looked like logs, but then suddenly began to move — a description that has recurred in Ogopogo sightings through the years. Captain Thomas Shorts saw a 5 m creature from the deck of his steamer in 1890. In 1914, a strange animal carcass with flippers and a long tail was pulled out from Lake Okanagan, measuring 1.5 m and weighing 180 kg, but it was most likely a manatee. A 1925 report in a Vancouver newspaper popularised the Okanagan monster legend and led to the usage of the Ogopogo name.

In 1959, a group on a motorboat noticed what appeared to be a large creature trailing them. They turned and headed toward the creature, getting within 50 m and seeing its snakelike head before it disappeared under the waves. Another group reported a similar experience in 1968, saying they chased after Ogopogo at 65 km/h but were unable to keep up.

Also in 1968, Arthur Folden captured film footage of the supposed creature with his 8mm movie camera. Although extremely hazy, the single minute of footage appears to have recorded an aquatic animal between 15 and 20 m in length, quickly diving and surfacing and leaving a wake behind it. Some observers claim to see a head, a tail and a three-humped back, but these features are indefinite. Fearing public ridicule, Folden kept the film private until 1970, when he turned it over to the local mayor. The subsequent public screening sparked an immediate sensation, with the film being largely discredited as fake or inconclusive. Discouraged, Folden disappeared from the media's reaches and refused further examination of his film.

In 1976, Ed Fletcher produced a series of Ogopogo photographs, showing a long, humped object barely breaking the water's surface. No features are distinct, and the apparent creature could simply be a formation of waves, or a bumpy log, although Fletcher and his eyewitnesses claimed the head of Ogopogo was unmistakably visible.

The primary argument against the existence of Ogopogo is the lack of convincing photographic evidence. Nonetheless, the vast number of sightings reported for over a century — and their high degree of consistency — makes Ogopogo one of the most conceivably real lake monsters. Described again and again as an elongated, serpentine creature with no increased thickness in the middle body, about 12 to 20 m in length, Ogopogo sounds very much like a *zeuglodon,* a prehistoric whale. But there are two problems with that hypothesis: zeuglodons are thought to be extinct, and being air-breathers, they would have to surface with far more regularity than what the bashful Ogopogo has exhibited.

17. Manipogo

Canada's Lake Manitoba holds claim to a sea monster legend that dates back to 1908. The creature was dubbed *Manipogo* in 1957, the name echoing British Columbia's Ogopogo. (Following the same tradition, neighbouring Lake Winnipegosis boasts Winnipogo.) The described characteristics of Manipogo are roughly similar to those of Ogopogo, leading some to theorise that they are specimens of the same species — perhaps surviving prehistoric *zeuglodons.*

Louis Belcher and Eddie Nipanik reported seeing a huge, serpentine creature swimming across Lake Manitoba in 1957. After other sightings came in, the Manitoba provincial government launched an official expedition to search for Manipogo and learn what threat such a monster might pose. This was followed by a more comprehensive scientific investigation in 1960. In both cases, nothing extraordinary was discovered living in the lake.

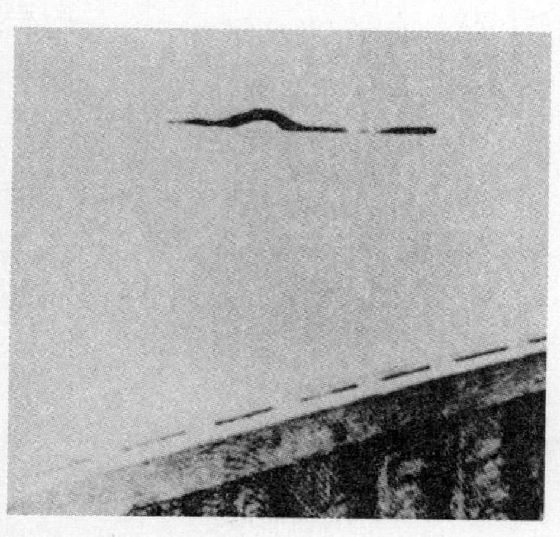

In August 1962, two fishermen named Richard Vincent and John Konefell took a photograph of what they claimed was Manipogo. Vincent said he thought the creature was "a large black snake or eel which was swimming with a ripple action... it was about 30 cm in girth, and about 3.5 m of the monster was above water. No head was visible." The men estimated that the humped portion of the creature seen in the picture was about 60 cm long, and guessed that they took the photo from about 50-75 m away. They attempted to pursue Manipogo in their motorboat, but despite their 10-horsepower motor they weren't fast enough to keep pace, and he got away.

Vincent and Konefell's photograph has convinced some observers, including zoologist James A. Macleod of the University of Manitoba. "If that isn't the monster," Macleod said of the fishermen's picture, "I'd like to know what the deuce it is." But the twisting object in the photo is too indistinct to draw any meaningful conclusions from, and no further significant evidence of Manipogo has yet been offered.

18. The Queensland Monster

In December 1964, French photographer Robert Serrec was on vacation in Queensland, Australia, when he took the photograph of a lifetime — or faked it. He was paddling rowboats with a group of family and friends in shallow waters off Hook Island, near the Queensland coast, when he says "a bizarre creature appeared beneath the waves."

Serrec described the monster as an enormous, dark-coloured snake with the shape of a giant tadpole. It had a huge reptilian head and a slender, waving body that stretched to about 20-25 metres. Serrec said there seemed to be a wounded area on the creature's back. One of Serrec's photos presents a very clear and striking image that distinguishes it from the average blurred, murky sea monster's picture. Serrec also shot some movie camera footage underwater, but it did not turn out with any distinct detail.

Serrec's photo and his story have been widely discredited as a hoax. The main argument against the photo is that it is simply *too* clear — it looks so perfect and so overly "real" that many experts believe, ironically, that it must have been staged. It is also extremely difficult to judge the scale of the supposed creature. The position of the tiny man in the rowboat above the monster creates the visual impression that the monster must be gigantic, but it could actually be a small prop photographed at very close range, with the rowboat off in the far distance.

19. The Mann Hill Monster

Sea monster stories don't always end with the inconclusive despair of "the one that got away." There are frequent instances of these unknown beasts getting caught or discovered, although generally these captured specimens ultimately turn out not to be so mysterious.

In November 1970, a huge, rotting corpse washed up on the shore of Mann Hill Beach in Massachusetts. About 6 m long and weighing several thousand kilograms, the carcass had a long neck and what appeared to be flippers. One observer described it as resembling a camel without legs. To many, the creature looked very much like a *plesiosaur*, and therefore might be evidence that the supposedly extinct prehistoric species was alive and well in Loch Ness and elsewhere.

But scientific analysis showed that the monster was in fact the badly decomposed body of a basking shark. Although commonly found in the oceans, the basking shark has a strange, oddly shaped body that is unfamiliar to the average person. Their dead bodies tend to rot away in such a manner that the remains roughly resemble a plesiosaur, and match the popular conception of a Nessie-type creature.

Unidentified marine corpses like the Mann Hill Monster are sometimes called *"globsters,"* being basically globs of barely recognisable flesh and bone. The original globster washed up on a beach in western Tasmania in August 1960, and was eventually identified as the partial corpse of a whale. But on the whole, basking sharks are the guilty party in globster cases more often than any other aquatic species.

20. Zuiyo-maru Plesiosaur

One of the most prominent cases of a misidentified *globster* reported as a sea monster took place in April 1977, on board a Japanese fishing boat named the *Zuiyo-maru.* About 50 km off the coast of Christchurch, New Zealand, the trawler's nets snared a huge animal carcass of an indeterminate sort. The crew hauled the monstrous body out of the ocean and up over the deck, and at first they thought it was a rotten whale. But after a closer look, they weren't so sure.

The creature was 10 m long and weighed about 1800 kg. It had a snakelike head at the end of a long, slender neck, making it seem rather unlike a whale. Some crew members commented that it looked like a giant turtle without a shell, and it also had a strong resemblance to a *plesiosaur.* Although they recognised that this was possibly a scientific discovery of historical proportions, the crew of the *Zuiyo-maru* agreed that they had to throw the carcass back into the sea. If they kept the decayed creature on board, it could contaminate the catch of fish that was more valuable to them than any scientific find. Besides, the awful stench coming off the carcass was unbearable.

But as the crew attempted to wrangle the beast back into the water, it unexpectedly fell through the supporting ropes and crashed to the deck. This delay allowed Michihiko Yano, the ship's assistant production manager, the opportunity to take some quick measurements of the creature and shoot several photographs. Yano also had the forethought to excise samples of "horny fibre" from one of the fins of the carcass, to help in later identifying the creature. Then the stinking monster was thrown overboard, for good.

The fish company for which the *Zuiyo-maru* worked was very excited about the sea monster story and the striking photos, and they publicised the event with great fanfare. The resultant hoopla created a national craze over sea monsters throughout Japan, encompassing wind-up toy replicas and a postage stamp depicting a plesiosaur, which is what many scientists initially proposed the creature to be. But analysis of Yano's photos and tissue samples led to the conclusion that the creature was a decomposed basking shark.

Despite this solution to the *Zuiyo-maru* mystery, there are those who persist in believing that the carcass was actually a plesiosaur or some other unknown animal, citing supposed inconsistencies in the creature's skeletal structure or other characteristics. These indefatigable believers can always point to the fact that the crew rashly threw the precious evidence overboard, and thus we will never know absolutely for sure what it was. Or at least, that gives us a reason to pretend not to know.

21. Malaysian Dragon

In a sort of miniature reproduction of the *Zuiyo-maru* plesiosaur phenomenon, Malaysian fishermen made a strange catch in May 1996 in waters near the northern resort island of Langkawi, Malaysia. At a depth of 50 m, their nets pulled in a mysterious 8 m skeleton that the crew believed might be a dragon.

"We were shocked and did not know what it was," said Lim Yow Sam, the captain of the ship. "We thought it was a dragon and we were very scared to haul it in."

Some reports indicated that superstitious fear of the dragon caused the crew to throw the carcass overboard, but they kept it and turned it over to fisheries department officials. Initial press reports suggested that it looked like the remains of some modern dinosaur, sparking wild speculation on the Internet.

"The teeth and vertebrae seem mammalian, yet the head seems reptilian," noted cryptozoologist Karl Shuker, on the basis of examining a photograph of the skeleton. "If it's a whale, the mouth seems unusually large. The remains would allow a marine biologist to identify it clearly had one studied it, but the detail in the photo is ambiguous. For example, if that is a flipper near the head, it is most probably a type of whale."

And indeed, that's what it was. A killer whale, to be exact, according to Dr. Mohamed Azmi Ambak, a fishery taxonomist who examined the bones firsthand. Killer whales are very common in Malaysian waters despite the consternation this particular specimen stirred up. And thus did it happen that the *Malaysian Dragon* turned out to be a whale of a tale.

22. White River Monster

From about 1915 to the late 1970s, residents of Newport reported seeing a monster in the White River. This monster, nicknamed *"Whitey"*, was described as being snakelike and at least 9 m long. Witnesses reported that it made a loud bellowing noise and had a spiny backbone. Many reports were made by fishermen and campers along the river. In 1971, two men reported that they saw three-toed tracks along the muddy river banks and at places where the trees and vegetation had been broken because of the monster's size. The creature was even photographed in 1971 by Cloyce Warren of the White River Lumber Company. Was the photograph really that of a monster? Arkansas legislators seemed to think so.

The most interesting part of this legend happened in 1973. The Arkansas State Legislator created the White River Monster Refuge along the area of the White River that runs adjacent to the Jacksonport State Park. They enacted a resolution which made it illegal to "molest, kill, trample, or harm the White

River Monster while he is in the retreat." Is this proof of his existence or just an attempt to draw tourists?

There are many explanations for Whitey. Biologists believe Whitey was actually a lost elephant seal. He somehow migrated incorrectly and ended up in Newport. Some townspeople believe that it was an elaborate plot to gain attention by farmers in the area. No one knows for sure.

The monster hasn't been seen much in recent years but many of the people living around the White River still believe he is there. Some think that he has died because the river has gotten shallower. You'll have to find out for yourself. There is a lot of monster memorabilia around White River—T-shirts, etc.

23. Giant Squid

Although the *Giant Squid* (*Architeuthis sp.*) is already known to science, and thus is not technically a *cryptid,* there is still very much we do not know about the Giant Squid.

The history of the Giant Squid probably begins with the legends of the *Kraken,* which was discussed by Bishop Pontoppidan. The Kraken was a legendary monster that was believed to be as big as an island. When people landed on it (mistaking it for an island), the Kraken would sink, killing everyone on it. Descriptions of the Kraken, saying that it had many arms on it, have led some people to think that the Kraken may have been an exagherated account of the Giant Squid.

Interestingly, there are accounts of beached giant squids dating back to the 1600s. Because of the chemical makeup of the Giant Squid's skin, it floats after dying, giving it a chance of being washed onto shore. Sperm whales were also reported to have puked up large tentacles while the whale was being killed, sometime before the Giant Squid was accepted by science.

A Giant Squid was seen by the *Alecton,* a French warship, in 1861. They managed to get a rope around it, though the body slipped off, except for it's tail. A Giant Squid attacked a small boat in 1873 but the crew of the boat managed to hack off some of it's tentacles and escape. One of the tentacles, which was 5.7 m long, was obtained by Reverend Harvey, who also later obtained another carcass. The carcass was given to Professor Verill, who then classified it and settled the issue of the Giant Squid's existence.

Since then, many other Giant Squids have been washed ashore and caught in trawling nets. The Giant Squid lives in the depths of the ocean, and if seen alive, is usually close to death.

There are a few accounts of Giant Squids attacking ships. In 1874, a Giant Squid pulled down a schooner, from which some of the crew managed to escape. During World War II (in 1941), after the *Britannia* had been sunk, 12 of the survivors were left on a small raft. At one point, one of the survivors was pulled down by a large squid, and (presumably) killed. Lieutenant R. E. G. Cox was grabbed by a tentacle, which let go and left a scar on him (the squid was probably about 7 m long). In the early 1930s, the a Giant Squid attempted to attack a tanker, the *Brunswick.*

We have virtually no information about the Giant Squid's habitat (except that it lives in the ocean), it's prey (although Sperm Whales are known to eat Giant Squid), or how long it lives. The maximum size of the Giant Squid is also unknown. The largest authenticated Giant Squid was about 17 m long, though there may be bigger squid. One reported sighting said that the squid was about 52 m long. Some Sperm Whales were reported to have scars from Giant Squid that were about 10 cm in diameter. If these were the actual size of the squid's tentacles, then the squid would be about 24 m long.

Only a few people have actually seen living Giant Squid, and even then the Squid were most likely dying. There have been attempts to film Giant Squid in their own environments, by using submersibles. So far these attempts have been unsuccessful, and the Giant Squid still remains as one of the most elusive sea creatures accepted by science.

24. Giant Octopus and Globsters

In several cases, carcasses were washed up on beaches. The carcasses bore some resemblance to gigantic *octopuses,* and were given the nicknames of *Globsters.*

One of the first known Globsters was sighted around 1896, near St. Augustine, Florida. It was a white rubbery lump, 6 m long, 2 m wide, and 1.2 m tall. It also had what looked like pieces of tentacles, which made it look similar to a giant octopus. The thing in St. Augustine came to the attention of Professor Verill, who confirmed that it was an octopus, and gave it the name *Octopus giganteus.* The carcass was further damaged when a storm took it out to sea and redeposited it on the shore. An attempt was made to move the carcass from the shore to protect it, and Dr. Webb cut some pieces of the carcass (much later, the pieces were tested by Roy P. Mackal, who concluded that they resembled an octopus's skin tissue). For some reason, Verill later said that it was probably part of a whale, though it in no way resembled a whale. Eventually, the carcass was taken back out to sea by tides.

The St. Augustine monster was not the only Globster to wash up. A similar blob was washed up in Tasmania in 1960; science ignored it for over 2 years, and then said it was a whale.

Another Globster washed up in 1968, in New Zealand, and again in 1970. Another Globster washed up on Mangrove Bay, in 1988.

Theoretically, the blobs could have been extremely rotted pieces of whale carcasses, though it is harder to explain away the tissue from the St. Augustine monster. Also, all of the blobs were extremely hard to cut, which is not similar to whale pieces. Moreover, the Globsters did not seem to have any of the bones or organs a whale would have.

The Giant Octopus seems to be one of the best supported cryptozoological creatures. Like the Giant Squid, the Giant Octopus is probably a deep water creature, and would only rarely be seen alive, though there are some recorded sightings. In 1802, Denys de Montfort reported an event, where a ship near Angola was attacked by a monster that tried to drag down the ship with its tentacles. The monster was stopped when the seamen started chopping off it's arms. A picture of the event shows a Giant Octopus, though the creature in the obviously exaggerated picture has tentacles that would have been about 9 m thick.

In 1951, a broken cable was brought up from 2160 m. The cable had half a kilo of tissue wrapped around, which may have come from an octopus.

In 1989, a group of people was in a boat off the coast of the Philippines, when they saw a tentacle go over the side of the boat. One person said he saw a head in the water, and that the tentacle was about 2.5 m long. The boat was capsized, and the people waded to the safety of shore.

25. El Chupacabras

The single most notable cryptozoological phenomenon of the past decade is undoubtedly *El Chupacabras,* the fearsome Goatsucker of Latin America. The legend of this livestock-slaughtering monster was born in small villages in Puerto Rico in 1995, and quickly spread to Mexico and Hispanic communities in the United States, ultimately becoming a worldwide sensation like no unexplained creature since the Bigfoot film of 1967.

El Chupacabras was preceded by a Puerto Rican monster known as the *Moca Vampire,* which had been reported in conjunction with a rash of UFO sightings in 1975. A number of farmers discovered animals massacred after strange lights appeared in the sky. Investigators examining the slain animals, which included ducks, goats, geese and cows, noted with astonishment that they had been completely drained of blood with almost surgical precision. The Moca Vampire was apparently never sighted firsthand, but perhaps whatever it was it possesses some connection to the creature that made itself known 20 years later.

In March 1995, the Puerto Rican towns of Orocovis and Morovis began to be plagued by some force that was mysteriously murdering their animals. The carcasses of goats, chickens and other small farm animals were reported to be thoroughly exsanguinated, with the blood often said to have been drained out through a single neat puncture wound.

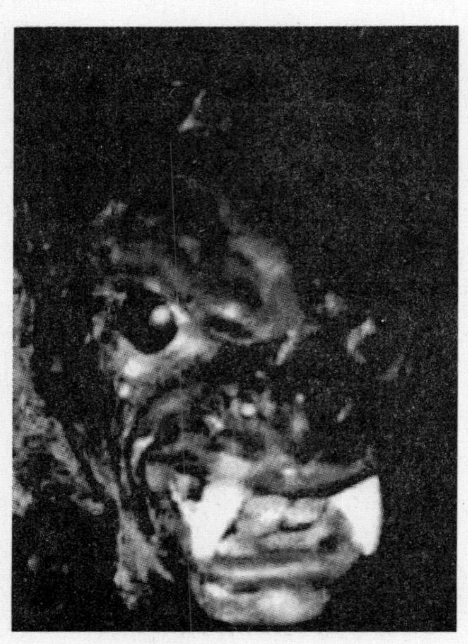

The first sightings of the creature were reported around September of that year. Madelyne Tolentino and other witnesses described the creature as a sort of a cross between a kangaroo, a gargoyle, and the pop-culture conception of the alien "Grey." It was said to be about 1.2 m tall, with a large, round head, a lipless mouth, sharp fangs and huge, lidless red eyes. Its body was small, with scrawny, clawed arms and webbed bat wings, and muscular hind legs that appeared to be built for jumping. The creature also had a series of pointy spikes running from the top of its head down its backbone. Paranormal investigator Jorge Martin drew a sketch based on these descriptions, which rapidly became the classic visual image of El Chupacabras, as the local media had dubbed the monster. The name, of course, is Spanish for ***"the Goatsucker."***

Sightings and slain livestock continued to be reported in various parts of Puerto Rico throughout the fall of 1995. The Goatsucker allegedly killed 11 goats in the town of San German, and on one occasion a group of townspeople said they chased the creature away as it was attempting to kill three roosters. In Canovanas, seemingly an epicentre of Chupacabras activity with more than 150 animal slayings reported in 1995, the town's Mayor Jose "Chemo" Soto sanctioned paramilitary patrols to hunt down the monster. Soto's political candidates accused him of pandering to his constituent's fears, and attempting to capture the anti-Chupacabras vote instead of the creature.

After December, there was a lull in Goatsucker sightings, which some surmised was because the creature withdrew to inactivity during the winter months. And indeed, come springtime El Chupa rose again — although this resurgence owed more to the mass media than to warm weather. In March 1996, a segment on the Goatsucker appeared on TV talk show *Christina,* the Spanish-language Univision network's very popular counterpart to *Oprah Winfrey.* The show drew a tremendous response, and Chupacabras updates became a regular feature of the program. This exposure spearheaded the migration of Chupamania into Mexico and the United States and, perhaps not coincidentally, also preceded the first sightings of the strange predator in these new lands.

Whatever else it may or may not be, El Chupacabras represents folklore in the modern age of electronic telecommunications. In the olden days, it took centuries for a legend like the Loch Ness Monster to be disseminated through generations at a creeping pace. The tales we tell now are really pretty similar, and it's primarily the speed of word of mouth that's changed. Television shows and news reports obviously anchored its public relations campaign, but more significantly, the Goatsucker is the first monster the Internet can call its own.

1995 was the year the World Wide Web began its explosion, and the Goatsucker just happened to be caught in the right cultural revolution at the right time. The famous Jorge Martin Chupacabras drawing infiltrated an unseen network of weirdness-watchers, and the story achieved iconic stature in Internet circles without the mainstream media needed to ladle it out to the masses. Chupacabras tales were meanwhile enthusiastically spread by Hispanic-oriented information sources. This generated a one-two punch of underground publicity, struck in two separate subcultures, and the Goatsucker phenomenon was running wild before the mass media even knew what it was.

At the height of the craze, there were probably a couple dozen *"Goatsucker Home Pages"* on the Internet. Some of them are still around today, including one at Princeton University that may legitimately be the original Goatsucker site. The web site of sensational radio host Art Bell posted an alleged photograph of a living Chupacabras, depicting a ridiculous creature later exposed as a statue from a museum exhibit. The photo nonetheless became a major touchstone of Chupa lore, fuelling American interest in the creature.

The first major American sighting of the Goatsucker took place in March 1996 in Miami, Florida. This just happened to occur shortly after the creature was featured on the *Christina* show, and that program just happens to be taped in Miami. In the predominantly Hispanic south Miami neighbourhood of Sweetwater, 69 various animals were reported slain overnight. The massacre included goats, geese, ducks and chickens, all of which bore wounds that looked like bite marks. The livestock were not drained of their blood, though, and police and investigating zoologists felt that the attacker was a large dog. The animals' wounds were consistent with canine bites, dog hair and dog footprints were found, and an entryway had been dug under a fence just as a dog would do.

Still, there was at least one eyewitness to El Chupacabras in Sweetwater. An elderly woman in the area described seeing a large, doglike creature. "It stood up on two legs and was hunched over like this with big arms and looked at me with these red eyes," she said before a phalanx of TV news cameras.

The Goatsucker reportedly struck Texas's Rio Grande Valley in early May. A goat belonging to Sylvia Ybarra was found dead with three puncture wounds on its neck. It was the pet of 19-year-old Ybarra, who called it Nena. Ybarra had recently seen news reports of El Chupacabras and was convinced that it was responsible for the killing, although no one saw the creature in this case. A veterinarian who examined the goat believed that it was killed by a dog.

Soon afterwards, in the predawn hours of May 9, the Espinoza family of Tuscon, Arizona reported encountering El Chupacabras at their home. Joe Espinoza claims to have found the creature outside his door, gesturing and mumbling and smelling terrible, "like a wet dog." It then entered the house through an open window and briefly sat atop Espinoza's seven-year-old son. The Chupa did not harm the boy, nor any animals, but the Espinozas claimed to find its footprints afterwards. Tuscon police, brought to the scene by a 911 call, believed the prints were actually those of one of the young Espinoza boys.

Is the Goatsucker really nothing more than a myth, transmitted by mass hysteria and modern communications? A lot of analysts think so, noting the possible sociological implications of the creature. Bloodsucking monsters are a common motif in the folklore of Latin American countries, and are thought to represent these cultures' sense of exploitation at the hands of wealthier nations. Others have suggested that the bloody imagery of Chupacabras attacks makes the creature a psychological personification of the AIDS epidemic, which has brutally ravaged the Hispanic population.

In any event, Chupa sightings have decreased in frequency since 1996, although the occasional report still surfaces from time to time. Whether the Goatsucker is real or not, we probably haven't yet heard the last of our weird *amigo* from Puerto Rico.

26. Mothman

Around midnight on November 15, 1966, two young couples were driving down a dirt road by an abandoned TNT plant near Point Pleasant, West Virginia. Roger and Linda Scarberry and Steve and Mary Mallette said they saw a strange grey figure standing near the plant's front door, with large red eyes that glowed in the dark and wings folded against its back. As the frightened couples sped away, the creature reportedly spread its wings and took off through the air in pursuit of the car. Even at speeds approaching 160 km/h, the bizarre flying "bird" kept up with them. It made a loud, high-pitched shrieking noise, and it flew without flapping its wings. The creature followed them all the way down Highway 62 to the Point Pleasant city limits before flying away.

The four witnesses reported what they'd seen to the Point Pleasant police. All of them remarked on the strangeness of the creature's huge red eyes, which seemed to be set right into the monster's shoulders or chest, as though it had no head. They also noted that the eyes seemed to be "hypnotic."

The Scarberrys and the Mallettes were not alone in having a strange encounter that night. At about 10:30 that evening, Newell Partridge was watching TV at his home in Salem, West Virginia, about 140 km from Point Pleasant. Partridge's television went blank with static, and he heard his hunting dog Bandit howling outside. Partridge went to look outside with a flashlight, and he saw two large red glowing circles that he thought were the eyes of an animal. Bandit went charging in the direction of the eyes, despite his master's calls for him to come back. The dog never returned.

The following day, Sheriff George Johnson announced the Scarberry and Mallette sightings to the press. Even though the descriptions uniformly seemed more similar to an owl or a big bird, a reporter named the creature *"Mothman"* after a villain on the then-current hit TV show, *Batman.*

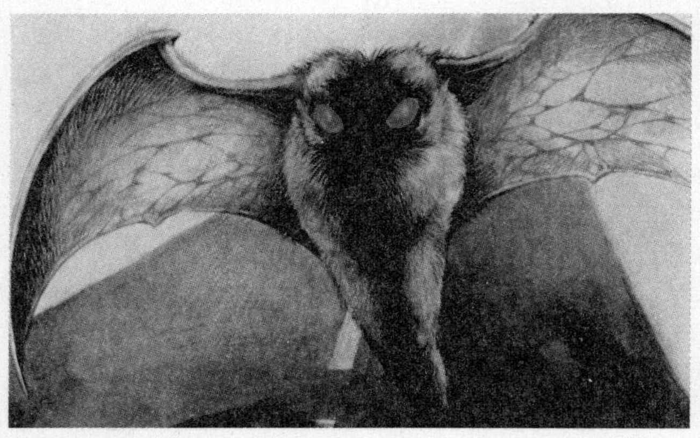

On that night of November 16, Macella Bennett was getting into her car after visiting friends in Point Pleasant, when she saw a grey figure with red eyes rise up on the other side of her car. She said it was taller than a man and had eyes in the middle of its headless torso. Bennett was so terrified she dropped her baby daughter, and her friend Raymond Wamsley picked up the unharmed infant before they dashed back into the house. They said the creature peeked through the windows at them, but by the time police could get there, it was gone.

Sightings of Mothman in Point Pleasant and other areas of West Virginia continued coming in for a period of about one year. The creature has rarely been sighted since November 1967, giving the impression that it was in Point Pleasant for a short time and then left for good.

The definitive chronicle of the phenomenon was recorded by author John A. Keel in his acclaimed book, *The Mothman Prophecies*, a half-journalistic, half-fiction novel based on firsthand investigations and interviews with the major eyewitnesses. Keel ties in the Mothman appearances with UFO sightings that were also reported in the Point Pleasant area, weaving a strange tapestry of extraterrestrials, ultraterrestrials, Men in Black, the CIA and a massive conspiracy of silence.

For a more mundane explanation of the Mothman case, it has been suggested that the witnesses may have seen sandhill cranes, a variety of large bird that can stand five or 2 m tall. These cranes are not normally found in West Virginia, but could conceivably migrate there from Canada. Another theory is that the creatures were simply large owls. In any case, it would take a tremendous amount of panic and fear for any one person's mind to perceive a normal bird as this menacing creature, and a large number of people would have to share the same misconception. This is just one of the reasons why Mothman is one of the strangest phenomena not only in cryptozoology, but also in the entire realm of the unexplained mysteries.

27. Jersey Devil

Even though it has seldom been sighted in the past 90 years, the *Jersey Devil* enjoys a level of popularity that few other cryptozoological entities can rival. The people of New Jersey consider the legendary creature an unofficial state mascot, and their NHL hockey team is named in its honour. The Jersey Devil was also featured in the third episode of *The X-Files* as the series's first ever *"monster of the week,"* and a Sony PlayStation game has turned the savage beast into the latest *"Sonic the Hedgehog"* video game character.

The Jersey Devil legend dates back to well before the Revolutionary War, and the details of its origin have become understandably vague and mysterious. The story generally goes that in 1735, a woman in the pine barrens of southern New Jersey gave birth to a cursed child. The mother's name is often given as Mrs. Leeds, but other accounts say her name was Mrs. Shrouds, and she lived in the town of Leeds Point. One version of the story indicates that the woman had 12 children, and when she found herself pregnant with a thirteenth, she angrily cried, "May the Devil take this one!" Other variations say that Mrs. Leeds was a witch, or that the Devil was the baby's father, or that she was simply the despised local slut.

Whatever the reason for her child's dire fate, it was born a hideous monster. Its freakish anatomy is most often described as the combination of a horse's head, the wings of a bat, cloven hooves and a serpent's tail. The newborn beast supposedly flew off into the woods of the pine barrens (after killing its mother and family, according to some accounts), where it has remained in hiding for hundreds of years. It was originally called the *Leeds Devil,* and in the 19th century it came to be known as the *Jersey Devil.*

In 1909, nearly two centuries after the creature's reputed birth, there came an unexplained rash of sightings that has been dubbed the Jersey Devil's "finest hour." In January of that year, the monster would seem to have gone berserk across eastern Pennsylvania and southern New Jersey, with about 100 people in 30 towns saying they saw it over a brief span of about five days. The first of these sightings took place on January 17 in Bristol, Pennsylvania, when Bristol postmaster E. W. Minister claimed to see a flying monster that had a piercing scream. The next day, a policeman in Burlington, New Jersey, said he saw a flying creature with glowing eyes. From the surrounding area, reports poured in of similar sightings and strange, unidentifiable hoofprints found in the snow.

On either January 19 or 21, Nelson Evans of Gloucester City reported seeing the Jersey Devil outside his home. "It was about a metre and quarter high, with a head like a collie dog and a face like a horse," Evans said. "It had a long neck, wings about two feet long, and its back legs were like those of a crane, and it had horse's hooves. It walked on its back legs and held up two short front legs with paws on them. It didn't use the front legs at all while we were watching. My wife and I were scared, I tell you, but I managed to open the window and say, 'Shoo!' and it turned around barked at me, and flew away."

The entire region quickly became consumed with a mass hysteria. Area schools and businesses closed in the interests of public safety, and newspapers and zoos placed bounties on the Jersey Devil's head. Con-artists began to get in on the action, as in the case of Jacob Hope and Norman Jeffries, who hoaxed a capture of the monster. They charged admission for a peek at a kangaroo they had disguised with green paint, feathers and antlers.

A dramatic showdown reportedly took place on January 21 in West Collingswood, when the town's fire department is said to have confronted the monster and sprayed it with their firehoses as it swooped menacingly over them. The next morning, a Mrs. Sorbinski of Camden said she saw the Jersey Devil attack her dog. This report marked the end of the 1909 rampage. There was one more sighting in February, and only a few scattered reports in the years since.

The Jersey Devil would most likely be nothing more than an obscure piece of colonial folklore today, if not for the unexplained sightings of 1909. No one can say what made so many people have such similar sightings if the monster was not real. The most reasonable explanation, unlikely as it may seem, is that the phenomenon was purely psychological, and mass hysteria led people to see something that wasn't there. Hoofprints and other evidence could have been faked or misidentified, and no animal could possibly move fast enough to cover the vast geographical area of the 1909 sightings. Unless, of course, there's a whole colony of Devils hiding out there in the Jersey pine barrens.

28. Loveland Frog

In May 1955, a man reported an unbelievably strange sight while driving home at 3:30 am in Loveland, Ohio, northeast of Cincinnati. He claimed to have spotted three bipedal reptilian creatures standing by the side of the road, and pulled over to watch them from his car for about three minutes. One of the froglike beings carried some type of bar or wand above its head, and sparks were shooting out of the device. The driver notified Loveland police of what he had seen, although no evidence of the creatures was later found.

Almost twenty years later, in March 1972, an unnamed Loveland police officer was driving on Riverside Road at about 1:00 am, travelling slowly because of ice on the road. Up ahead he saw an animal standing at the side of the road, which he first thought was a dog. As the cruiser's headlights fell on the animal, it rose upright from a crouching position, showing itself to be a metre tall with leathery skin and a head like that of a lizard or frog. The beast looked at the officer momentarily before jumping over the guard rail and heading for the Little Miami River down below. The officer returned to the scene with another policeman a few hours later, and they found scrape marks on the embankment where something had apparently slid down to the river.

Two weeks later, another unnamed Loveland policeman reported a very similar encounter. Driving on the same road, he saw an animal lying in the middle of the pavement, which he thought was either dead or dying after being hit by a car. He got out of his car to clear the animal to the roadside, when suddenly the animal jumped up and the officer saw that it was a strange froglike creature. It began to flee, limping as if it were injured, and headed over the guard rail towards the river. The officer shot at the monster as it went down the embankment, but apparently did not hit it.

Neither of the officers filed an official report of the weird creature, but word of their sightings leaked to the press, and the modern legend of the Loveland Frog was soon spread far and wide. A farmer in Loveland also claimed to see a froglike creature in March 1972. Investigators began to speculate on a connection with the 1955 sighting of reptilian creatures, and the possibility of a secret race of lizard men inhabiting Ohio's rivers. Some have suggested that the officers may have actually seen a Nile monitor lizard or a large iguana, which can be over 2 m in length. But if so, these reptiles would have to be escaped from a zoo or otherwise transplanted to the area, since they are not native to the region.

Abnormally large reptiles and reptile men have also been reported in other parts of the country, including the *"Lizardman"* of Wayne, New Jersey, and the *"Giant Lizard"* of Milton, Kentucky. The most celebrated successor to the Loveland Frog in recent years was the Lizard Man craze that swept Bishopville, South Carolina, in 1988. A man reported that a 2 m reptilian beast with red eyes and three-fingered appendages chased his car along a country road at over 40 km per hour. A large number of other sightings followed, and police officers discovered three-toed tracks. But ultimately, the only hard evidence the Lizard Man left behind was the fattened bank accounts of local bumper sticker and T-shirt vendors.

29. Dover Demon

On April 21, 1977, three 17-year-old boys were driving through the Boston suburb of Dover, Massachusetts, at about 10:30 pm. The driver, Bill Bartlett, saw in his headlights an animal creeping along a low stone wall by the roadside. At first he thought it was a cat or dog, but as he came closer he saw that it was like no earthly creature he'd ever seen.

Bartlett said, "It had a large head the size and shape of a watermelon, with no visible features except for two round, orange eyes. The rest of its body was thin and spindly, with long, extended fingers and toes that wrapped around the rocks of the stone wall as it walked. It was about a metre tall, with peach-coloured, hairless skin."

After his quick glimpse, Bartlett asked his two friends if they saw what they'd just driven past. As it turned out, they had been talking to each other at the moment, and didn't see the creature. They persuaded Bartlett go back for another look, even though he was so frightened he didn't want to turn around. They found nothing when they went back. Bartlett then headed home and made drawings of what he had seen.

That report alone would make for a pretty good monster story, but then something else happened. About two hours after Bartlett's sighting and a little over a kilometre away, 15-year-old John Baxter was walking home from his girlfriend's house when he saw a small figure walking towards him on the same side of the road. Baxter thought it was a neighbourhood boy he knew, and called out the boy's name. He got no answer. The two walked closer together until Baxter saw the other figure suddenly stop. It then ran off down a gully and climbed up to the opposite bank. Baxter followed and got his first good look at the creature, which he said had a large, round head, a thin body and long, grasping fingers and toes. Baxter watched the creature for a moment, then became scared and ran away from it.

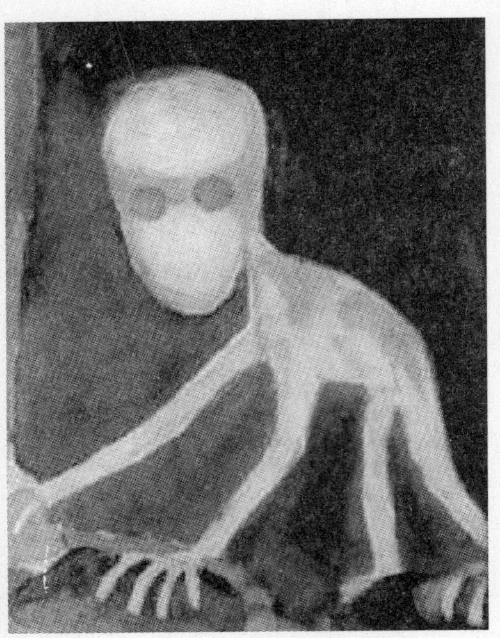

Baxter also drew pictures of what he had seen. Soon word spread of his and Bartlett's sightings, and when their stories and drawings were compared, it seemed that the two had seen exactly the same creature. By all accounts, Bartlett and Baxter had never met before, and there was no reason to suspect that they had conspired together on a monster hoax.

The day after the sightings, Bartlett told his 18-year-old friend Will Taintor about what he had seen. That night, Taintor was driving 15-year-old Abby Brabham home around midnight. Brabham claimed to see a creature matching the same description crouching by the side of the road as they drove past — even though she had reportedly not heard about what Taintor's friend had seen. Taintor also caught a fleeting glimpse of the creature.

Cryptozoologist Loren Coleman happened to be living in the Dover area at the time of these sightings, and was among the first investigators to tackle the case. It was he who named the creature the *Dover Demon,* a name that was picked up by the press and has stuck with the creature ever since. Interviews with the witnesses convinced Coleman that their encounters were genuine, despite their youth and the weirdness of what they had seen. It has been suggested that the animal they saw may have actually been a newborn horse, but that seems an unlikely solution. The Dover Demon remains one of the most baffling and compelling of all unexplained creature sightings.

30. Mongolian Death Worm

The desolate Gobi Desert is said to be the home of a mysterious, deadly creature called *Allghoi khorkhoi,* also known as the *Mongolian death worm.* It is described as a fat, bright red snakelike animal measuring 0.6 to 1.2 m in length, which is vividly likened to a cow's intestine. In fact, the name *Allghoi khorkhoi* means "intestine worm." The death worm is so feared among the people of Mongolia that many consider the mere mention of its name bad luck, and it is attributed with the dramatic ability to kill people and animals instantly at a range of several metres. It is believed that the worm sprays an immensely lethal poison, or that it somehow transmits high electrical charges into its victims.

The foremost investigator of the Mongolian death worm is Czech author Ivan Mackerle, who first learned about the creature from a female student from Mongolia. After Mackerle told her about a diving expedition he had made in search of the Loch Ness Monster, she told him in a conspiratorial whisper, "We, too, have a horrible creature living in Mongolia. We call it the *Allghoi khorkhoi* monster, and it lives buried in the Gobi Desert sand dunes. It can kill a man, a horse, even a camel."

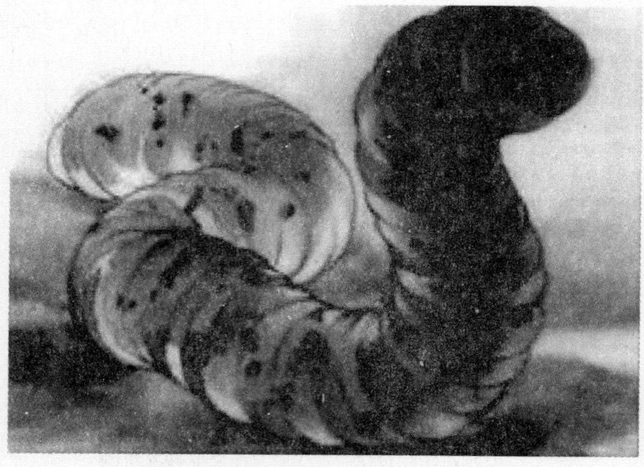

Intrigued, Mackerle set out to learn more about this Mongolian monster, but information on the topic was very hard to come by. As he would soon learn, this was primarily because most Mongolians were afraid to discuss the death worm. In addition, the Communist government of Mongolia had kept the nation isolated, and outlawed the search for *Allghoi*

khorkhoi, which the government considered a "fairy tale." Communism collapsed in Mongolia in 1990, and the new political climate provided Mackerle the freedom to mount an expedition to the country's desert wastes to hunt for the worm.

Mackerle and his colleagues befriended some Mongolian nomads who were willing to discuss the death worm, after a couple of bottles of Mongolian vodka loosened their tongues. They said that the worm squirts an acidic liquid that immediately makes anything it touches turn yellow and corroded. The nomads also said that the colour yellow attracts the *Allghoi khorkhoi.* They told a story of a young boy who was playing outside with a yellow toy box, a death worm crawled inside. When the boy touched the worm, he was killed instantly. The boy's parents found his body and a wavy trail leading away in the sand. They knew what had happened and followed the trail to kill the worm, but it killed them instead.

Mackerle's group also encountered an old woman named Puret who reluctantly agreed to discuss the worm. "I have never personally seen the *Allghoi khorkhoi,*" she said, "but I have heard much about it. It is said to move about under the sand, and when it wants to kill someone, it moves half its length out of the sand. It starts to inflate. The bubble on its body keeps getting larger, and, in the end, the poison squirts out from it."

If the Mongolian death worm is real, it's highly unlikely that it is literally a worm. Annelids and similar invertebrates are unable to survive in a brutally hot and dry climate like the Gobi desert, because their bodies cannot retain moisture and they would rapidly die of dessication. It has been suggested that *Allghoi khorkhoi* might be a worm that has adapted some sort of cuticle membrane to hold in moisture, but a more reasonable candidate would be a snake or other reptile.

Mackerle has posited that the creature might be a skink, a strange variety of lizard whose nondescript head is hard to distinguish from its tail. Skinks also live buried under desert sands, but they have four stubby legs and scales, unlike the reportedly smooth-bodied death worm. Mackerle has also suggested that it could be a type of lizard called the worm lizard, although that species is not poisonous. Among lizards, only the Mexican beaded lizard and the gila monster possess poisonous venom, but they do not squirt it, and their venom definitely is not instantly lethal on contact.

Another possibility is that the death worm is a member of the cobra family called the *death adder*. This species has an appearance similar to the descriptions of the *Allghoi khorkhoi,* and it does spray its venom. But although the death adder could conceivably survive in the Gobi environment, they are found only in Australia and New Guinea.

Then there is the matter of the death worm's reputed ability to kill its victims from a far distance, without even shooting venom. Some have proposed that this might be performed with an electrical shock of some sort. This hypothesis might have arisen from an association with the electric eel, but the eel and all similar electricity-discharging animals are fishes, and none of them could have the ability to live on land, much less in a desert. Most likely, the "death from a distance" component of the *Allghoi khorkhoi* legend is an exaggeration based on fear.

And the death worm itself is most likely a fiction based on some desert-dwelling snake or reptile, which is not truly as deadly as its reputation would suggest. Unless, of course, it really is a species that's never been identified before. Admittedly, any animal that can instantly kill anyone who tries to observe it would stand a good chance at escaping scientific classification.

31. Mokele-Mbembe

Some people believe there's no need to clone DNA preserved in prehistoric amber in order to return dinosaurs to the Earth, on the grounds that the creatures never went fully extinct. For hundreds of years, stories have been told of surviving dinosaurs in the jungles of central Africa. The earliest written record comes from a 1776 book in which Abbe Proyhart described seeing giant, clawed animal footprints in west central Africa, tracks that he claimed were a metre across.

In 1913, a German expedition in the Congo met a group of pygmies who described an animal they called *mokele-mbeme,* which means "one who stops the flow of rivers." They said this beast was about the size of an elephant or hippopotamus, with a long, flexible neck and a long tail like an alligator's. They claimed that the animal would attack and kill any humans that got too close to it, but it would not eat them, because of its strictly herbivorous diet. Similar descriptions have been given time and time again throughout central Africa, consistent with a sauropod or other small dinosaur.

Numerous expeditions have been mounted in search of mokele-mbeme, with mixed results. In 1980 and 1981, monster-hunter Roy P. Mackal headed explorations into the Likouala and Lake Tele regions of the Congo, as reputed hot spots of dinosaur sightings. Mackal documented a number of past eyewitness accounts, including one exciting story of how one mokele-mbeme was attacked and killed. Pascal Moteka, who lived near Lake Tele, said that his people had once constructed a barrier of stakes across a river to keep the giant beasts from interfering with their fishing. When mokele-mbeme tried to break through the barrier, the assembled villagers managed to kill it with spears. Celebrating their triumph, the people butchered and cooked the carcass, but everyone who ate the dinosaur meat reportedly died soon afterwards.

Mackal never saw the creature himself, although he says he did have one close call. One day while paddling down the Likouala River in dugout canoes, his group heard a loud "plop" sound and a large wake splashed up on the far bank. The pygmy guides cried out frightfully, *"Mokele-mbeme! Mokele-mbeme!"* Mackal and his colleagues believed that only a large animal diving under the water could have caused such a wake, and since hippos are not present in the Likouala area, they felt that they narrowly missed seeing the elusive dinosaur.

Marcellin Agnagna, a Congolese biologist who had accompanied Mackal on his searches, led his own expedition in 1983. Agnagna claimed to have a firsthand sighting of a mokele-mbeme as it waded in Lake Tele. He described it as having the long-necked form typically attributed to the creature, although he could not see its legs or tail, which remained underwater. Agnagna had a movie camera, but he later reported that there was little film left when the creature appeared, and he began filming it without realising that the lens cap was left on. Thus, even though he says he observed the animal for about 20 minutes before it submerged and vanished, Agnagna was sadly left with no photographic evidence — a convenient circumstance, sceptics might say.

In 1992, a Japanese film crew captured some of the best photographic evidence of a mokele-mbeme ever presented. They were filming aerial footage from a small plane over the area of Lake Tele to obtain some panoramic landscape shots for a documentary. They noticed a large shape moving across the surface of the lake and leaving a V-shaped wake behind itself. The cameraman zoomed in and got about 15 seconds of the object in motion before it dive under the surface.

The resulting footage is very jumpy and indistinct, but it shows a vertical protuberance at the front of the object that could be a long neck. A second, shorter projection could be a humped back or possibly a tail. If the object is not a dinosaur, it's difficult to say what animal it could be, since a crocodile would not have two such protrusions above the water, and an elephant would not submerge in the way the object does. The explanation that makes the best visual match is actually two men paddling a canoe, although the object's speed is too fast to be a non-powered boat.

The existence of dinosaurs in central Africa is unlikely, but not a total scientific impossibility. According to cryptozoologist Karl Shuker, "If dinosaurs could exist unknown to science anywhere in the world, the Likouala is where they would be."

32. Beast of Bodmin Moor

One of the most popular subcategories of current cryptozoology, particularly in Britain, is the investigation of what are known as *alien big cats,* or *ABCs.* The word "alien" here is meant to denote large felines that are "out of place," rather than "extraterrestrial" — for instance, a common panther or leopard found somewhere that conventional zoology says it should not be. *Fortean Times* co-editor Paul Sieveking reported that ABC sightings have recently become the hottest topic of interest among the magazine's British readers. Perhaps one reason for the popularity of alien big cats is that they are a more tangible quarry for monster-hunters than more fantastic creatures like Bigfoot. And there are sightings aplenty, totalling around 300 in 1996 alone.

In the early 1990s, reports began to circulate of alien big cats in and around Cornwall, in southwestern England. Bodmin Moor became a nerve centre of these sightings and reports of inexplicably slain livestock, and the alleged leopardlike felines of the region came to be popularly known as *"the Beast of Bodmin Moor".* All the talk of dangerous wild cats led Great Britain's Ministry of Agriculture, Fisheries and Food to conduct an official investigation in 1995. The study's findings, released on July 19, concluded that there was "no verifiable evidence" of exotic felines loose in Britain, and that the mauled farm animals could have been attacked by common indigenous species. The report did concede, though, that "the investigation could not prove that a 'big cat' is not present."

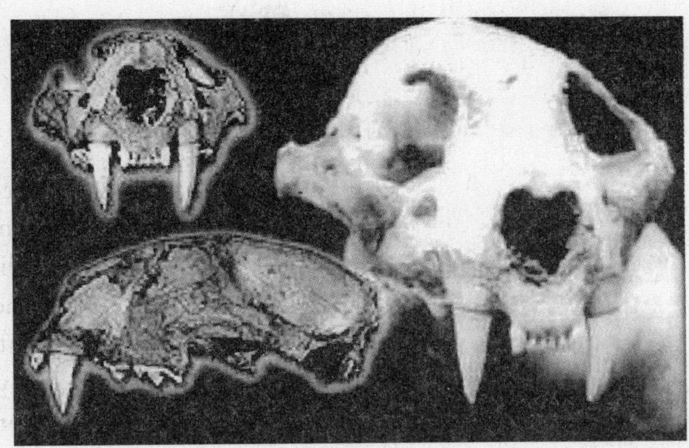

On July 24, less than a week after the government report, a boy uncovered a startling piece of evidence in Bodmin Moor. Fourteen-year-old Barney Lanyon-Jones was walking with his brothers by the River Fowey at the southern edge of the Moor, when he saw a strange-looking object bobbing in the river's current. Barney thought it was an oddly-shaped rock until he pulled it out of the water, and discovered that it was a large cat skull. Measuring about 10 cm wide and 18 cm long, the skull was missing its lower jaw but possessed two sharp, prominent incisors that suggested a leopard. The story hit the national press on July 31, a well-timed counterpoint to the official denial of alien big cat evidence in Bodmin Moor.

The Lanyon-Jones family turned the skull over to London's British Museum of Natural History for verification.

Dr. Ian Bishop, the museum's assistant keeper of zoology, examined it and determined that it was a genuine skull from a young male leopard. But he also found that the cat had not died in Britain. Bishop concluded that the skull had been imported as part of a leopard-skin rug.

The back of the skull had been cleanly cut off in a way that is commonly used to mount the head on a rug, and there was an egg case inside the skull that had been laid by a tropical cockroach that could not possibly be found in Britain's climate. There were also fine cut marks on the skull indicating that the flesh had been removed with a knife, and the skull had slightly begun to decompose only after a recent submersion in water.

This was not the first time the skull from a mounted trophy had stirred confusion in the search for alien big cats. In 1988, two teenage boys found a skull on Dartmoor that was never turned over for official study, but the missing back of its skull made many experts suspect a rug-based origin. In 1993, the Natural History Museum had previously identified a large cat skull found in Exmoor as being part of a work of taxidermy.

Doug Richardson, assistant curator of mammals at London Zoo, has suggested that a prankster may be planting these skulls on the moors in hopes of misleading their discoverers.

Sightings of the Beast of Bodmin Moor still continue. In October 1997, officials from Newquay Zoo claimed to identify pawprints left in mud to the south of Bodmin Moor as the fresh tracks of a puma. Soon after that discovery, an alleged photograph of the Bodmin Beast materialised, which seemed to show an adult female puma that looked like it could be pregnant. The authenticity of this piece of evidence remains unconfirmed.

33. Thylacine

Imagine a bizarre animal that appears to be half wolf and half tiger, with a head like a large dog's, hindquarters like a hyena's, and tiger stripes covering only the rear half of its body. Let's say this beast also has a long, rigid tail and a pouch like a kangaroo's, except that the pouch opens backwards. It sure sounds like a mythical mishmash of different species, similar to a *jackalope* or *minotaur,* but guess what? This creature is a real animal. Or at least, it was.

The *Thylacine* was also known as the *Tasmanian Tiger* or *Tasmanian Wolf,* but it was neither feline nor canine. It was a carnivorous marsupial which was thought to be a distant relative of the opossum. Like so many marsupials, the thylacine was exclusively native to Australia. The species seems to have been driven off the continent's mainland about 12,000 years ago, probably because of a losing battle against dingoes. The thylacine found refuge on the island of Tasmania, which was once connected to the continent by a land bridge, and became the only place on Earth where thylacines were found.

In the 19th century, European settlers on Tasmania verified the thylacine as a destructive menace responsible for slaughtering sheep and other livestock. Both government and private agencies offered bounties to have them killed. Thylacines were exterminated at a rapid pace, with the animal's strange appearance making it an easy target and public hatred fuelling the hunt. By the early 20th century, the thylacine was nearly wiped out and no longer a significant threat, and yet the killing continued. Bounties on the animal were officially ended in 1909, but the thylacine was still being hunted down as late as 1930.

The people of Tasmania finally realised that the thylacine was virtually extinct. In 1933, the last known specimen was captured and kept at the Hobart Zoo, where it was named Benjamin. In 1936, Tasmania declared thylacines a protected species, but only two months later, Benjamin died in captivity. On that day, the thylacine officially became extinct.

But soon after Benjamin's death, the new sightings began. People began seeing thylacines in wild areas across Tasmania, engendering belief that the reports of its extinction was premature. Some experts are willing to concede that a small number of thylacines may survive in hiding somewhere in Tasmania, but despite a vast number of sightings and discoveries of alleged thylacine tracks, no concrete evidence of the species's survival there has yet been produced.

And as if thylacine sightings in Tasmania aren't strange enough, there's also plenty of thylacine sightings outside Tasmania. The island of Tasmania was the sole and isolated habitat of the animal for thousands of years, and now there are reports that the creature is still alive in other places — most commonly on the Australian continent, but in other parts of the world as well.

In 1981, the Australian government hired professional tracker Kevin Cameron to investigate sightings of a strange animal in Western Australia. Cameron soon reported that he saw the animal and said that it was a thylacine. In 1985, Cameron produced a series of alleged photographs of a living thylacine. The pictures were initially convincing, but analysis cast doubts on their authenticity: the animal's head was never shown, its body never changed position, and the photos were taken from wide variety of angles that were inconsistent with Cameron's story of a 20- to 30-second encounter. Cameron's photos are generally judged to be of a fake or stuffed thylacine, an explanation which raises the possibility that Cameron may have killed a living thylacine and staged these photos, to avoid the government's $5,000 fine that would apply to the killing of a thylacine, which is still listed as a protected species.

The thylacine has also been recently spotted alive and well as far afield as Indonesia and England. These reports have no more credibility than the average Bigfoot sighting, or maybe even less, since there is no documented data on Bigfoot's exclusive habitats. But the thylacine has become one of the favourite topics of modern cryptozoology, even attracting the attention of famous adventure-seekers like Walt Disney, Sir Edmund Hillary, and Ted Turner, who have all searched for the creature. The thylacine truly is the world's most common extinct animal.

34. Thunderbird

The strange case of the Thunderbird is unique in the study of unknown animals, because it contains two mysteries in one: the search for a long-lost and probably nonexistent photograph of the creature has virtually eclipsed the search for the creature itself.

The Thunderbird is a part of Native American mythology in tribes of the Pacific Northwest and the Great Lakes. These giant, birdlike creatures were said to generate lightning from their eyes and to cause thunderclaps by flapping their massive wings in the sky. There are countless sightings on record of the revered supernatural entity, or a huge bird fitting its description, both by Native Americans and the "white man."

The most celebrated Thunderbird encounter took place in 1890, on the desert sands of what was then the Arizona Territory. Two cowboys had a bizarre confrontation which has varied widely in the telling, but the gist of the story is this: they saw a giant flying bird, shot and killed it with their rifles, and carried its spectacular carcass into town.

A report in the April 26, 1890, Tombstone *Epigraph* listed the creature's wingspan as an alarming 50 m, and noted that the bird was about 28 m long, about 1.25 m around at the middle, and had a head about 2.5 m long. The beast was said to have no feathers, but a smooth skin and wingflaps "composed of a thick and nearly transparent membrane... easily penetrated by a bullet." Perhaps the hardest part of this story to swallow is that two horses could manage to haul a dead behemoth like this for any distance.

Sounds like a typical tall tale of the Wild West, and that's probably what it is. But it apparently does contain a kernel of truth. In 1970, Harry McClure claimed that as a boy he knew the two cowboys from the story later in their lives, and they had told him a different version of the events. McClure said the giant bird they saw in the desert actually had a wingspan of more like 6 to 9 metres. The two riders shot at the creature, but it was out of range. Their spooked horses refused to chase it, so the men rode into town empty-handed, carrying only news of the one that got away.

The Tombstone newspaper printed its highly embroidered version of the cowboys' sighting, which was spared from fading into obscurity by its inclusion in a 1930 book on the Old West. In 1963, the story came to the attention of writer Jack

Pearl, who revived the tale for an article in a pulpy men's adventure magazine called *Saga.* As if the *Epigraph* report hadn't spiced up the facts enough already, Pearl liberally embellished the encounter into a dramatic rip-snorter entitled "Monster Bird That Carries Off Human Beings!"

Pearl pushed the date of the encounter back to 1886, and he described the witnesses as two prospectors who killed the bird and proudly showed off their trophy in Tombstone. Pearl also added some extra conflict by telling of how a second Thunderbird snatched up a heckler who had ridiculed the prospectors and flew away with him in its talons. But Pearl's most significant editorialisation was this: he said that the *Epigraph* newspaper story had run with a photograph of the giant bird's carcass, nailed up to a wall with its mighty wingspan unfurled, and a number of men posing next to it for scale.

This part of the legend, the Thunderbird photo, has taken on a life of its own. Pearl's fictional account of a photograph of Old West settlers with a big dead bird was picked up and repeated time and again, multiplying and evolving just as it had before Pearl ever got hold of it.

In time, people who heard the story began to believe that they had previously seen the photo with their own eyes. Somehow, people felt convinced that they had once marvelled at the strange picture in some old book or newspaper, often noting that they didn't realise the significance of the photo at the time, and regretting that they had not kept it. The details might differ from one recollection to the other, with some recalling the bird had feathers and others saying it looked more like a pterodactyl, and some thinking the bird was nailed to a wall and others remembering that it was held with wings outstretched by a large group of men. But no matter what the specifics, each person feels certain his or her memory is true.

Many have reported that they saw the Thunderbird photo in *FATE Magazine, National Geographic, Grit,* or some other similar publication, but entire archives of these periodicals have been searched, and no Thunderbird discovered. The experts in the cryptozoology field are no less susceptible to Thunderbird recollections than the common layman, with Ivan T. Sanderson and John A. Keel among those who claim to have once held the photo in their hands. Some accounts of seeing the photo are amazingly precise and hard to disregard. Larry Thomas told *Strange Magazine* that he saw the photo in a library in the early 1980s, as an adult, in a thin hardcover book of photography from the Old West. He says that he was so fascinated by the picture that he looked at it dozens of times over a four-year period, and he even checked the book out once so he could take it home for his wife to see.

It's difficult to tell someone that an experience as vivid as that never really happened, but what is the alternative? What's the word with the Thunderbird?

The best explanation for the phantom photo phenomenon is that these are memories of things that never existed. It might simply be that people have read descriptions of the cowboys and the giant bird that were so colourful and evocative that their imaginations created a near-tangible mental image of the scene. As the controversy surrounding "false memory syndrome" has demonstrated, the things we think we recall can be distorted by external suggestion, mismatched fragments of things that did happen, and maybe even debris from the collective subconscious. Some might view this line of reasoning as party-pooping scepticism, but if it is correct, what it reveals about the mysteries of the human mind is way more interesting than any big bird could ever hope to be.

35. Beast of Exmoor

In the spring of 1983, Eric Ley of South Molton, Devonshire, England, lost over one hundred of his sheep in a period of two and a half months. He noticed the killer of the sheep did not attack its prey from behind as would a dog or a fox, but ripped out their throats much like a lion taking down its prey. The creature thought responsible for the killings is described, by those who have seen it, as a huge black cat. Initial reports of people sighting the *Beast of Exmoor* actually began in the early 1970s, but did not gain public attention until the slaughters occurred at the Ley Farm.

Many theories have been formed since the Beast of Exmoor began surfacing. Most people think the huge cats are actually large dogs or some other form of misidentification. Other less popular theories say the creatures are intruders from another reality.

36. Kangaroos in the United States

Just like puma and panthers being spotted in Australia and Europe, kangaroos have also been seen not within their original habitat. Kangaroos have been seen often in the United States since the mid 1960s. A man had reported a kangaroo on his porch early one morning in Chicago on October 18, 1974. Patrolmen Byrne and Ciagi were astonished to find a 1.5 m kangaroo in a dark alley around 3:30 am. Not knowing what else to do, Byrne tried to handcuff it. The animal was not going to go quietly as it started to scream, then Ciagi was kicked in the shins and the kangaroo escaped down the street.

That was not the only sighting in Illinois. A couple of weeks later on November 2, in Plano, Illinois, two separate groups of witnesses reported seeing a kangaroo almost at the exact same time. Within another couple of weeks, sightings have occurred in Lansing, Illinois; and Rensselaer and Carmel, Indiana. Then on November 15, back in Chicago, a kangaroo was seen in a vacant lot. The witness said it was 1.5 m tall and "black all over, except for the stomach and face, which were brown." The last known sighting took place on November 25 in Sheridan, Indiana, when a farmer, Donald Johnson, spotted a kangaroo on a deserted rural road. Johnson stated: "It was running on all four feet down the middle of the road." When it noticed Johnson, it leaped over a barb-wire fence and into the field.

In Wisconsin, 1978, a photograph was taken of a kangaroo. The picture was admittedly not very good, but clear enough to make out the creature. The kangaroo was first spotted in Waukesha on April 5, 1978. On April 24, there were other sightings at Pewaukee Township, Brookfield Township, and around Waukesha. Near Menomeonee Falls, two men had taken two pictures of a kangaroo, and was said that this creature could possibly have been an escapee from a private animal collection or zoo, living wild.

Out-of-place animals, such as kangaroos, are rarely captured and they seem to disappear as mysteriously as they appear. It seems only few citizens see them and it is usually from a distance. However, in May 1979, a kangaroo seen in Nashua, New Hampshire, was caught and found to be a wallaby (an Australian marsupial similar to a kangaroo, but smaller) that had escaped from a carnival that had recently left town.

Other sightings of kangaroos, outside of their habitat, were also seen in New Brunswick, Nova Scotia and Ontario, Canada; around Morange-Silverange in France, and on the northern border of Hungary.

37. Beast of Gevaudan

From 1764-1767, a creature that became known as the *Beast of Gevaudan* began terrorising southeastern France. The first sighting happened in a forest where a woman saw a wolflike beast that was driven off by her cattle. Not long afterwards, people's bodies were being found torn apart, including a girl whose heart was torn out. Supposedly, people had shot at it with little effect to the Beast. Some hunters shot it repeatedly, after which it limped off. The killings resumed in a few days.

King Louis XV, sent a group of soldiers to kill the Beast. The soldiers thought they had killed it, but the killings continued after they left. Apparently, people even left entire villages out of fear of the Beast. Finally, in June 1767, the Beast was killed by Jean Chastel, who had fired 2 silver bullets into it (believing it was a werewolf). All in all, about 60 people were killed by the Beast of Gevaudan. The corpse of the Beast was taken throughout France, and then buried after it started to rot.

The Beast of Gevaudan definitely existed, though no one is sure just what it was. A Paris newspaper said that the Beast was bigger than a wolf, had red fur, and a black coloured back. The paper also suggested that the Beast was a cross-breed of a wolf and a hyena. It has been suggested that it was a wolf, though such a killing spree is uncharacteristic of wolves. There is also the more sensational idea that it was a werewolf, as believed by the peasants of the day. Unfortunately, we will probably never be sure what it was, as the body was never preserved and it is now over 200 years since the killings.

References

1. Unexplained! Jerome Clark, Visible Ink Press, 1993.
2. Mysteries of the Unknown: Mysterious Creatures, Time-Life Books, 1988.
3. Bigfoot, John Napier, Berkley Publishing Corporation, 1974.
4. Alien Animals, Janet and Colin Bord, Stackpole Books, 1981.
5. Unexplained Mysteries of the 20th Century, Janet and Colin Bord, Contemporary Books, 1989.
6. Lucy's Bones, Sacred Stones and Einstein's Brain, Harvey Rachlin, Henry Holt and Company, 1996.
7. "The Abominable Showman," Ian Simmons, Fortean Times #83, November 1995.
8. "Planet of the Ape Suits," Loren Coleman, Fortean Times #86, May 1996.
9. "Not So Abominable Now," Loren Coleman, Fortean Times #89, August 1996.
10. "Debunking a Racist Hoax," Loren Coleman, Fortean Times #90, September 1996.
11. "Oo-be-doo, I Want to Be Like You," Fortean Times #95, February 1997.

12. "Fortean Follow-Ups: Just a Chimp off the Old Block," Fortean Times #99, July 1997.
13. "Suits You, Sir!," Loren Coleman, Fortean Times #106, February 1998.
14. "Clash over funding for rodent remains led to 'missing link' fraud," Roger Highfield, Electronic Telegraph report, May 23, 1996.
15. "The orange ape that walks like a man," Nicholas Hellen and Jonathan Leake, The Sunday Times (London).
16. "Two Yowie incidents reported in Australia," Joseph Trainor, UFO Roundup, September 21, 1997.
17. "Hollywood admits to Bigfoot hoax," Mike Lewis and Tim Reid, Electronic Telegraph report, October 9, 1997.
18. "'Distant cousin' of man found in Indonesia," Nando.net report, October 11, 1997.
19. The Encyclopaedia of Unsolved Mysteries, Colin and Damon Wilson, Contemporary Books, 1988
20. Mysteries of Mind, Space & Time: The Unexplained, Volume 1, H. S. Stuttman, Inc., 1992.
21. In the Wake of the Sea-Serpents, Bernard Heuvelmans, Hill and Wang, 1968.
22. Mysteries of the Unexplained, H. G. Carlson, Contemporary Books, 1994.
23. "Status Report: Lake Monsters," Mike Dash, Fortean Times #102, September 1997.
24. "Dragon Ahoy!" Fortean Times #89, September 1996.
25. "It Ain't Nessie-ssarily So!," Jonathan Downes, Enigma Magazine #4, 1997.

26. "Research shows Loch Ness monster unlikely to be too monstrous," UPI report, December 29, 1993.
27. "Skeleton of Sea Monster Excites Fishermen," Reuters report, June 14, 1996.
28. The Mothman Prophecies, John A. Keel, Saturday Review Press, 1975.
29. The Pine Barrens, John McPhee, Farrar, Straus and Giroux, 1968.
30. "Not as Simple as ABC," Paul Sieveking, Fortean Times #83, October/November 1995.
31. "Jersey Devil Walks Again," Loren Coleman, Fortean Times #83, October/November 1995.
32. "Dinosaur Caught on Film?," Mike Dash, Fortean Times #86, May 1996.
33. "How Many Goats Can a Goatsucker Suck?," Scott Corrales, Fortean Times #89, September 1996.
34. "What's Behind the Hispanic Panic?," Loren Coleman, Fortean Times #94, January 1997.
35. "Thunderbirds Are Go," Mark Hall, Fortean Times #105, December 1997.
36. "In Search of the Killer Worm," Ivan Mackerle, FATE Magazine, 1996.
37. "Menagerie of Mystery," Karl P. N. Shuker, Strange Magazine #18, Summer 1997.
38. "Wherever you are, beware of the beast," Paul Sieveking, Electronic Telegraph report, May 24, 1997.
39. "Beast of Bodmin is alive and breeding," Sean O'Neill, Electronic Telegraph report, October 18, 1997.